Dedication

But God! is dedicated to everyone that finds themselves in a wilderness situation, wondering how they will make it through and how they will make it out. To those who are reaping from what they have sown and finding the consequences of their actions less than favorable and just a step above being unbearable. To those who were chosen to go out amongst them and compel them to come but would rather pass on the assignment and give it to someone else. To those wondering and asking God why…why He will not give them a miracle of escape. This book is for you.

For those kicking against the prick, trying to do it their own way instead of yielding to the will of the Lord for their lives, for those who have yet to surrender…this book is for you. God is in control, and He knows the plans He has for you. This book "BUT GOD" will hopefully show you that when you put it in God's hands and allow Him to work in you, with you, and through you…it truly works out for your good, regardless of the circumstances or whereabouts.

When the time is right, I, the Lord, will make it happen. The LORD our God is Faithful and True Always. He will perform the counsel of His WORD accurately because He makes All Things Beautiful in His Time.

— Isaiah 60:22 (NIV)

Foreword

I am honored to have been asked to write this foreword. I gather the prayers, thoughts, wishes, and desires of my entire family as I pen these few words. I have had both the privilege and challenge of watching Alicia grow, slip, rise, fall, evolve, regress, overcome, and become the powerful woman of God she is today. Her life has been filled with peaks and valleys-BUT GOD! It is because of her connection to God, her power source, she is able to write this book and stand on its truths. It is because of God's lifelong lessons to her and through her I know those who read this book will be blessed and encouraged.

A true extrovert, Alicia is willing to share the "ugly side of pretty". She pulls back the velvet curtain of her beautifully complicated life and allows all who will to see the beauty and blessings along with the blood, sweat, and tears that have brought her safe thus far. BUT GOD! May those two powerful, pivotal, life-altering words resound in your spirit as you journey forward with Alicia. Yes. Life can be unyielding, unforgiving, and unloving, BUT GOD! Thank you, Alicia, for allowing God to use your life to bless others and remind us all that no matter what life holds for us, as long as we can declare and decree, "BUT GOD!" we have a way out, a way over, and a way through.

Your Proud & Loving Sister,
Marva Ceaser Dew
Author, *The Queen's Rules*

Table of Contents

Introduction

How could this be happening to me? I mean if it were one, five, ten years ago I would understand. Back when I was living an ungodly, unbecoming, unproductive, and unhealthy lifestyle, then it would have made sense. This should not be happening to me now...now that my life has changed for the better. Now that I am saved, in the church and actively working in ministry, now that I have repented and turned from my wicked ways. Now that I am trying to pull others out of the bowels of hell and into the kingdom of heaven. Why now?

I know we will reap what we sow. I know there are consequences to our actions. What I did not know is that after you repent and come out of darkness into His marvelous light...those consequences do not dissolve into thin air. So here I stand; saved, sanctified, filled with the Holy Ghost, and speaking in unknown tongues. I was water baptized, on fire for the Lord...and about to enter my own fiery furnace, my very own lion's den. I was facing the raging sea in front of me while the perpetual, persecuting, prosecutors, were breathing down my neck trying to alter my future of freedom.

Just when it seemed as if I were down and out, the wind shifted and favor, blessings, and miracles began appearing out of nowhere. When the dust cleared it was evident my crooked paths were made straight divinely...and no one could have made this way out of no way...But God!

The System

The first week of June, my pastors decided after one of our many prayer and consecration sessions, they would visit the members' homes and come against any unclean spirits, bless the premises, and pray God's favor there. When it was my turn for the visit, I happened to be there alone. My mother, whom I lived with at the time, along with my two sons were gone for a visit somewhere.

The home was clean, scented candles were lit, gospel music was playing softly on the radio, and I was preparing a light and healthy snack for my pastors to enjoy when the doorbell rang. I hurriedly answered, invited, and welcomed the Apostle and Prophetess in, and after brief chatter, we began to bless and rededicate the home to the glory and honor of God. As for me and my house (well my mothers' house), we shall serve the Lord. The entire visit took no longer than twenty minutes tops. As we were wrapping up and bringing our visit to an end and they were about to exit, the Apostle stopped in his tracks. He turned around toward me and said, "I have a word for you."

"Okay," I said and sat down on the nearest sofa.

He said, "I am not sure what this means, but God said the same system that holds you captive is the same system He will use to set you free." After relaying the message, he looked somewhat puzzled and asked me if I knew what that meant. With tears forming in my eyes and snot sliding downward and being sucked up before it exited the nostrils, I nodded my head yes.

I began to tell them of my previous visit with my probation officer, and how she explained that I had a warrant out for my arrest and that instead of her calling the police to get me on that day, she told me to go and get my affairs in order. She advised me to find someone to keep my children, someone whom I truly trusted. I was to write and notarize a letter that would give them temporary custody in case I had to spend any period of time being locked up in jail or prison. She stated having this document would give that person the authority to enroll them in school, take them to medical appointments, and have the legal right to make important decisions concerning them. She also told me to let my employer know I would be leaving, and said I should ask my family to help me find and retain a lawyer if it was at all possible.

She went on to say that she did not know why she was allowing this except it felt like the right thing to do. Before I left her office, she also told me that when I came back in a month, I should have on white socks and a plain cotton bra and panties in white or beige color. I agreed I would, although I did not understand why at the time. (This last part I just shared with you; I did not share with my pastors as I was retelling the story).

My female pastor Faye just looked at me with this concerned half-cocked smile. James, her husband, and our Apostle asked, "So what do you want to do?"

I said, "Run. I want to take my boys and move to another state."

He said, "You can do that, but you will always be looking over your shoulders for one, and two, that is not God's will for you." He went on to say he did not know how long I would have to stay incarcerated in jail or if I would have to face a prison term; God had not revealed that to him or any additional facts for that matter. He said, however, he did know that God would be with me and that I would come out victorious and free.

To be honest that was little comfort. I remember thinking that my way sounded better. Nevertheless, I believed God, and if He said He would be with me and bring me out a free woman, then so shall it be. Even though I did not have a clue where to begin…remember I was preparing to get ghost… things had shifted with me during that visit, and I now had to ready my mind that I would soon be going to jail.

Pastor Faye hugged me and as I hung on for dear life, she assured me that she and the church family would help my mom with my boys and that they would be there for me every step of the way. She held my hand, and we stood in a circle as she prayed a prayer that shot through the sky, parted the clouds, entered heaven's gates, landed in the throne room at God's feet, and then flowed into His nostrils. I cried, we embraced again, and after more words of encouragement, they left, leaving me to slump on the sofa and cry until my head began to swirl.

Sometime later, I gathered myself together and sighed in an act of submission and obedience to the directives I was given. I was going to go through the process and let God be God in my life.

I had two and a half weeks to prepare for this next unknown chapter in my life. Two and a half weeks to get my affairs in order. Two and a half weeks to let my family know what was about to happen. Two and a half weeks to spend as much time as possible loving on my two sons and making awesome memories. Lastly, I had two and a half weeks to try and get God to void this plan of incarceration and set me free miraculously without me having to be arrested.

I echoed Jesus…Father if it is possible, let this cup pass from me…nevertheless, thine will be done. Long story short, it was not His will for the cup to pass me by. Who knew in order to continue forward, I would have to confront the demons of my past? Nobody but God.

And I will lead the blind in a way that they do not know, in paths that they have not known I will guide them. I will turn the darkness before them into light, the rough places into level ground. These are the things I do, and I do not forsake them.

— Isaiah 42:16 (ESV)

The Dream

When I went to sleep that night, I was extremely nervous because I knew there was a warrant out for my arrest, nevertheless, I was tired but just could not get comfortable enough or make my mind stop wandering enough to fall asleep. I did not know if the police would knock at my door at any moment and if they did, who would be there to take my sons? I certainly could not have them going to a shelter until they could locate one of my family members. All of this and more was racing through my head, and I could not stop it on my own. Fear had a grip on me, and I could not shake it no matter how I tried to divert my attention to other things.

I had no choice but to call on the One who is able to give me peace that surpasses all my understanding. I went before His throne in prayer, I prayed in the natural at first, and then I prayed in the Spirit in unknown tongues until I fell asleep. It was a deep sleep and before I awakened in the morning, I had an amazing dream.

I was sitting amid the sky on a wide seated swing that had green vines where the hand poles should be, with my feet dangling in the air, although I could not see them. When I looked down all I could see were white puffy clouds gently moving in the cool but perfect breeze while surrounded by an amazing blue sky. When I looked up, I saw more of the same and I felt a calm like never before, so I held on to those vines, tilted my head back, and began swinging back and forth like I did when I once was a young girl. Not a care in the world, I was relaxed and enjoying the serenity of just being.

From out of nowhere I felt a presence and could see out of my left peripheral vision the tip of a vibrant gold wing rising out of the clouds beneath me. Not afraid I waited to see the manifestation of what was ascending, and it was the most handsome male I had ever laid eyes on. He was strong and solid in stature, his hands were massive, and he looked like a giant. His wings were humongous, and I could not see where they ended, they were so prodigious. His skin was a golden bronze and it was glistening as if he were soaked in baby oil. He had on the whitest gown imaginable with gold roped twists around the collar and the material around the wrists of his pure white robe moved in the breeze.

As I stared at him, he asked, "Do you know who I am?"

"No, I stated, should I?" He smiled, and when he did, I could have melted. His teeth were flawless, and fresh snowy white, and the sound he made when he spoke penetrated deep into my hearing down to my soul and spirit.

He said, "I am Michael, the Angel."

I turned abruptly on that swing seat so that my body was now facing him, and I asked, "Michael the war angel?" He confirmed that was exactly who he was, and I said, "But you are Black," and he laughed such a warm yet powerful laugh.

He then asked, "Do you know why I am here?"

No, I said, still in dismay that Michael the war angel was Black because I heard an evangelist on television say when he saw him, he was white with blue eyes.

Anyhow, Michael, the war angel said, "I came to teach you how to fight."

Wait, what? I know how to fight. I had been fighting one way or another most of my life, but I did not tell him that. I said, oh, all right, as if I understood what he was talking about. I looked around to see if anyone else was around and seeing this. If any-one else could witness what was going on so when I told this story they could back me up, but there was no one.

When I turned back to ask Michael the war angel how, what, and when he was going to teach me, he was already gone. I looked down and could not see him; I saw nothing but clouds. When I looked up, he was nowhere in sight. Looking to the left or right, Michael was nowhere to be found. He vanished as mysteriously as he appeared, leaving me with only those few words to think upon: "I came to teach you how to fight".

When I woke up and pondered on the dream, I had many questions, so I again went into prayer and asked God what that dream meant. He did not answer me with the answer I thought I needed, nor did He explain in detail what Michael the war angel was talking about, all He said was, "Remember the dream, it shall speak for itself."

I had no idea what I was about to face in the days and months to come. It was not until I was in jail that I understood the dream I experienced in the early morning that day would become the foundation I would have to learn and stand upon. The new way of knowing how to fight would be in the spirit realm.

This spiritual fighting would allow me to maintain my sanity, remain in control, and be the witness I was chosen to be in a place so filled with darkness — a place where His Omnipotent, Omniscient, and Omnipresent Light would be desperately needed. Fighting in the Spirit would be instrumental and the outcome would always be favorable if and when I obeyed the leading of the Holy Spirit.

Who knew the dream I had was to enlighten me that where I was going I would need to fight in the Spirit. Where I was headed, I would have to permit His Holy Spirit to increase and lead me because that would be the only way I would come out victorious. Who knew indeed…But God?

I do live in the world. But I do not fight my battles the way the people of the world do. The weapons I fight with are not the weapons the world uses. In fact, it is just the opposite. My weapons have the power of God to destroy the camps of the enemy. I destroy every claim and every reason that keeps people from knowing God. I keep every thought under control in order to make it obey Christ.

— 2nd Corinthians 10:3-5 (NIRV)

Day of Surrender

As I rode to the probation office with one of my good friends, who also happened to be one of the ministers at my church, along with my oldest son, my stomach was in knots. I had already been told by my probation officer on my last visit that I had a warrant out for my arrest. She was supposed to let the authorities know I was there that day, but instead allowed me to go home and put things in order. She told me without doubt when I came back for my next visit, she would have to call the police.

My probation officer said she would upon my arrival let them know I was there, and they would arrest me at her office. This was that visit. I had no idea what procedures this arrest would entail, how long I would have to stay in jail, if I would be sentenced to Prison, if I could be bailed out, and the when's and how's and where's and what-ifs were consuming my mind.

My son, Durrell (truth), who was twelve at the time, was playing a game in the backseat. He seemed to be minding his own business, but I could tell he was staring at me. There was a sense of tension in the car, even though upbeat music was playing and cool air was blowing in our faces. I was holding back the tears because I had no idea when I would be with my children again, when I would hear their voices or hold them or share my love with them again. My youngest son, Trenton (truth), who was not with me at the time was only two years old.

I remember thinking I would do anything for this not to be happening and I inwardly asked the Lord to give me a miracle and not allow this to happen.

Once we arrived and I checked in, while waiting on the probation officer to call me back, all I could do was look at my son. How could I get him to understand that I had to go away for a while, for something I had done in my past a few years before? I told him that I would not be coming back home with him that day, and he dropped his head and began twisting his hands. I told him that he would be staying with his granny and brother and that she and my family would take great care of him until I came home.

He forced a smile and said, "Don't worry. I'll take care of everything and everybody until you come home." He hugged me so tight, and I do not know if he was trying to give me strength or receive strength from me. I gave him money and asked my friend to please take him to get something to eat of his choice once I went to the back, and she agreed. I told him to keep the remaining money and use it for himself and his brother because he was in charge. The smile he showed upon hearing that gave me the strength I so desperately needed.

When the probation officer called me to the back, I stood and grabbed my son and hugged him as tight as I could once more. Tears streamed down my face as he tried wiping them away while telling me it would be all right and not to cry. I left him with my friend and walked through the doors without turning back to look at him, knowing if I did, I would have fainted from the heartache. I could hear him saying he loved me as the door began to close.

Upon entering her office, she told me to have a seat and she would be back shortly. She was going to retrieve the police. She exited her office for a brief time, and when she returned there were two male officers with her. They explained they were there for my arrest for a probation violation. I never let on that I already knew. I was instructed to stand up and place my hands in front of me. It was at this time one officer put handcuffs on me and read me my Miranda rights. The other officer signed papers for the probation officer to release me from her caseload and into their custody and authority.

One police officer held me by the arm as the other opened the door. The probation officer informed me that she would call my family members on file and tell them I had been arrested. She would tell them how to contact the jail for more information within a few hours. I thanked her and then I was escorted down the back stairs to a hallway and out of the building.

It was a bright, sunny, warm day and I remember looking up at the sky as the officers led me across the street toward the county jail. Suddenly, I heard my son calling for me. As I looked around, he was standing by the car, waving aggressively. In unison, the police officers told me to keep moving. I did as instructed, but yelled out, *"Mommy loves you, son!"* And that was the end of that. I was escorted around the corner into a parking area that led to the entrance of the jail.

I was taken to the front desk where I was told to take off any jewelry, empty my pockets, and take my hair ties out. This was the beginning of my booking process. I realized I had lost my right to object and if I wanted to do this smoothly, I had to comply with the orders given. My money was counted and placed in an account they assigned to me, later to be known as my "book." My wallet and personal property were placed in a manila envelope with my name and a "spin number" which would soon be required whenever I stated my last name to any officer. From there, I was fingerprinted, patted down, and then placed in a large holding cell where I would wait for hours upon hours.

This holding tank had two phones on the wall, immediately upon entering the room on the left side. I could see two open commodes placed behind a two-foot wall directly to myt right, cement benches that went around the circumference of the room, minus the bathroom area where the smell was fetid, and the entrance to the room where the pay phones were hanging on the wall. Women were spread out all over, most were sleeping with their heads against the wall behind them or bent over with their heads resting on their chests or laps.

The head against the wall was the position I took, that way I could see who was coming and going, as well as see when one of the phones became available so I could let my family know where I was being held. I desperately needed to know how soon they could get me a lawyer and get me out of this place. The jail was more than I could have imagined, and not in a good way.

I was a young Christian at the time of that arrest, and trust me when I tell you, the idea that I could possibly have an assignment in that place of sorrow was the furthest thing from my mind.

I was concerned with me, myself, and I. I had no idea what lay in store for me during my stay. I had no clue that being incarcerated would be instrumental in my life, that it would shine a light on my shortcomings, my passion, and my purpose. I never imagined jail would catapult me into a closer walk with God, as well as reveal a calling I had in my life. Who knew that situation and transition would be the answer to something I'd longed for since I was a child? Who knew…But God!

"For I know the plans I have for you," declares the Lord, "plans to prosper you and not to harm you, plans to give you hope and a future."

—Jeremiah 29:11 ESV

Stripped and Shamed

Finally, eleven hours after being booked in and waiting in an overcrowded, unventilated, damp, and musty holding cell where they handed out a hunk of peanut butter between bread, and an apple as a symbol of a meal, they called my name to line up so I could be moved to the next phase of the process. I was escorted to the showers with fourteen females and told to grab a plastic bag, disrobe down to my birthday suit, put my clothes in the bag, and prepare to be strip-searched.

I thought to myself. *This will be the most humiliating experience I will ever have to face.* I went to one of the guards and informed her I was on my cycle. That did not matter to her one iota, not in any way, shape, fashion, or form. I was instructed to follow directions and get naked and wait in line against the wall like everyone else.

When it came time for them to intrusively search me, the guard told me to open my mouth and lift my tongue. She then proceeded to stick her gloved finger in my mouth and do a sweep all around my teeth and gums. I was then ordered to lift my breasts, and then bend forward and grab my butt cheeks, and spread them open. I could have passed out from that embarrassment alone, but that was not even the worst part. The guard then told me to pull out my tampon, throw it in the trash and come back so she could check to make certain I was not hiding anything in that crevice. When I say they do a body check, that is exactly what I mean. They check every hole and area available from head to toe.

The indignity I felt at that time was indescribable, yet I had no choice but to comply. Refusal to do so would be detrimental to me. Refusing an officer's command would result in an infraction being added to my file, it would mean being put in the worst tank to show the officer's superiority, as well as other negative consequences that I did not want to find out about.

Next, I was pointed to the open showers where other females were standing under the streaming water. I approached those dirty showers where I had to stand barefoot under freezing water to cleanse myself. Then, because one of the females had crabs, we were all sprayed with some type of mist from a hose. I was later told by another inmate it was a delousing spray. I remember standing with my head under the water in an attempt to hide my tears, and somehow that bitterly cold water did not feel so brutal anymore.

After washing off, some of us were given back our bras and panties, but only if they were plain in color, and of cotton blend. Anything else was labeled as unfit because it could lead to temptation on the units. Thank GOD I had on all-white cotton undergarments. I had heeded the advice my probation officer had given me and whispered a word of thanks for her willingness to share.

At least this was in my favor, and I thought things were looking better. That thought was short-lived because before putting my underwear on I asked one of the guards for a tampon or pad. The guard looked at me and smirked, she told me to grab some tissue and use that, and to be grateful they still had some because I was not at a five-star hotel. I have never in my life associated toilet paper with comfort and luxury; nevertheless, I waddled over to the stalls with my legs tightly clenched to avoid leaving a trail of spotted blood droppings. As I rolled the tissue around my hand and placed it where needed, I closed my eyes briefly in an attempt to erase the embarrassment I felt with having to do this and the disgust I was feeling towards the dehumanizing organization called the justice system. More than ever, it became blatantly clear I was in over my head and had no idea what I would be facing.

I then got back in line to receive the orange outfit that would become my new attire. I was sized up by one of the guards, who then handed me a top and bottom wrinkled pair of clothing. I went to a corner and proceeded to put them on. But, to add another level of insult, neither piece would fit. So, I went back to one of the oh-so-unhelpful impolite guards in an attempt to get a bigger uniform. I was faced with the guards laughing at me in unison. "That is all we have, *madam,*" one of them said "You will have to wait to see if we have any bigger ones come in once you get to your floor."

Another one added. "We will check the men's unit, they usually have some big ones." This comment caused the three compassion-lacking guards to laugh once again. I was told to get back in line, to which I asked if I could have my clothes back until they found me a uniform. This question sent them into hysterics for a moment and then the name-calling and cussing began.

One of the guards stepped out and came back shortly with a thin, raggedy, cheap knockoff of what was supposed to be a wool blanket, which she threw my way. "Put this on and line up!" she snarled. "You will get the uniform when we give it to you. Now get in line, fatty!"

There I was, ashamed and at the back of the line, trying to conceal my body as best I could. Next thing you know, we were being marched down a long corridor that cut through the men's trustee section near one of the kitchens. I had to walk through this dorm section with a tattered piece of blanket wrapped around me. I felt as if I would stop breathing. I wondered if this was how Jesus felt when they mocked Him and marched Him through the town. Dramatic, I know, but I was so unimaginably uncomfortable and abashed.

The guys were whistling and making lewd remarks, and may I remind you these were the trustees. I put it in my head that they had not seen females in so long and that it had nothing to do with my body being exposed in different areas because of the fraction of material I tried to strategically place to cover the most vulnerable parts of my anatomy. Head down, tears of anger falling from my eyes, I kept moving, never looking around or behind me. I was trying to get wherever they were taking me as quickly as possible, only it was not so quick. We had quite a ways to walk, plenty of people to pass, and elevators to ride before I made it to the cell unit where I would be housed.

As soon as they assigned me to the first dorm, the one I would come to view as my new accommodations, I was brought an orange uniform that fit. I had just been told which cell I would be designated to stay in, and the bars had just slammed shut. I genuinely believe the problem was not that there was no orange attire to fit me, but was instead an ungodly assignment, a direct attack because I was a Christian in a not-so-Christian place about to wreak havoc in the enemy's camp. I believe this was satan's attempt to show his authority in that place of doom and gloom and was his way to alter the plans God had for me to complete.

Who knew that horrific act of humiliation would only catapult me into seeking God that much harder? Who knew indeed... But God!

For our struggle is not against human opponents, but against rulers, authorities, cosmic powers in the darkness around us, and evil spiritual forces in the heavenly realm.

— Ephesians 6:12 (NET Bible)

My Ultimate Fail

It was three thirty in the morning when I heard them yell my name, and the names of the other women who were going to court that morning. "Ladies, you have five minutes!" With that, the cell doors swung open, which meant we had exactly five minutes to get ready and line up in the day room when the guard opened the bars. Whatever you did not have on or in your possession when the guard came was too bad for you, and if you were not in line, depending on the guard, you would have then missed your court date.

Not I, no way, no how was I about to miss court. I believed GOD for my release, so I was the second one in line, with four minutes to spare, because I just knew this was the day I would be leaving this concrete jungle, my hostile companions, the stale food, and lack of privacy behind and going home. Home, where my family and friends would gather and wait to celebrate me with plenty of my favorite foods and drinks. Home, where once I finished taking a long, hot bubble bath I would put on a fresh array of colorful clothing of my choosing. Home, where I would be inundated with love and happiness.

From the tank, the other ladies and I were escorted around the corner where all the women had to line up against the wall for a cavity search and, yes, they again checked every cavity. From there we went to a large day room where all the women from the fifth floor that were going to court that day were being held. There were a hundred of us easily, and we waited not so patiently may I add, in an ice-cold room for forty-five minutes while they counted and checked us off.

Once again, the guard yelled for us to line up but this time in twos. After complying, we were told to shut our mouths. Anyone caught talking would automatically be taken back to their cells with disciplinary action against them that would be added to their case. Now, how did I end up next to the one woman who wanted to show that the rules did not apply to her? Out of nearly a hundred women, why was I selected to be paired with the woman who wanted to act out? She went on and on about how grown she was and what she would do if the guards did not have that radio, stick, and backup.

It did not matter to me in the least what she was saying over there, she might as well have been talking to a brick wall because I did not blink, smile, hunch, grunt, or anything. You would have thought I was blind, deaf, and dumb because I stared straight ahead as I inwardly pled the blood of Jesus and fervently interceded on my own behalf. I told you earlier no way and no how was I going to miss court. Well sure enough, a guard saw or heard that woman bumping her gums and called a male guard to come to escort her back to her tank. *Thank God,* I thought to myself.

Shortly after that incident, we were taken to our next checkpoint. At this station, we had to give our last name and spin number, move to another guard and open our mouths, lift our tongue and smile widely. We were then "scanned" with a metal detector and if cleared, we were told to walk down this extremely long hall, with guards posted deliberately along the way, in single file and wait at the line prior to the end of the hall before we reached the extremely large gray steel double doors. We complied with every instruction.

It seemed to me that I was right in the middle of the line. As we continued to wait in that long hall, all the guards began disappearing. Once they were gone, the women began talking amongst themselves. While I leaned back against the wall for a moment of silent prayer it came, as plain as the dew on a fresh fall day, a test of obedience from the LORD.

I heard that calm, smooth voice tell me to step out and ask if anyone wanted to be saved. I was to ask the women if they knew Jesus in the pardon of their sins and if He was their Lord and Savior. I looked to my right and then to my left and saw that all walks of women were on either side. I thought to myself, *You have got to be kidding, lose here Satan.*

I began to ponder in my intellect, but before I could fully complete the thought that beautiful voice asked, *When has Satan ever wanted to see anyone saved?*

There was no doubt in my mind, it was the Holy Spirit. *Why me and why now?* I wondered. I cleared my throat, took a deep breath, turned to the woman on my right. I said, "Excuse me, may I ask you a question?" After receiving permission, I asked, "Have you received Jesus as your Lord and Savior?"

She eagerly replied, "Yes, girl, and I was just praying to Him and asking for His favor in the courtroom. Will you agree with me on that?"

I did and added, "As God wills for your life, so be it unto you."

She said, "Amen, sister," and I exhaled feeling such great accomplishment.

Now my confidence was built up instantly. *That wasn't so bad at all,* I thought as I turned to the woman on my left, whose hair was some kind of a mess. It was all over her head, and was apparent she did not have time to use the comb that morning. Anyway, I started the conversation the same as before, "Excuse me, may I ask you a question?"

She said, "What?"

I asked again, "Do you mind if I ask you a question?"

"I heard you the first time," she snapped. "What do you want to ask me?"

"Oh, I apologize," I said. "Do you know Jesus as your personal Lord and Savior?"

Without hesitation, she interrupted with, "No I do not, and no I do not want to know Him and yes I want you to shut up talking to me now." She crossed her arms, then rolled her eyes, closed them and leaned back against the wall.

Guess whose air seeped quickly out of her self-inflated balloon? I turned around with my feelings hurt and thought to myself, *Her place is certainly secure in hell.* As if that thought was not demonic enough, the reason I thought that was not because the woman had rejected Jesus as her Savior, nope that was not it. It was because she had the nerve to dismiss me. *Who does she think she is? She evidently doesn't know who I am.* Can you say my pride was raw and in full effect.

That was not the end of it though, the LORD said, "You are to ask all the women if they are saved."

Come on now, I thought. *I have just been shut down by one woman and now I am supposed to step out in front of all of these women and offer salvation?* I leaned back, feeling sorry for myself like I was being bullied by God. You know I was in my flesh and temporarily having a moment of insanity. *Fine,* I thought, *let me get this over with.* As I started to step out and turn towards the women, a guard yelled for us to face the front and start walking. *Whew,* I thought, *well God you know I was about to do what I was told.* I was secretly happy we had to move on and imagined I just got over. Except God knows our thoughts before we even think them, so my secret was no secret at all, at least not to Him.

We were divided between eight holding cells, and I found a seat on the cement bench in the corner and put my head in my lap. I planned to stay in this position until my name was called. That was short-lived because the door opened and eight women were sent in. These women were all dressed in white, and they came from prison to be a witness about cases that were being heard that day in the county jail. Those cases that had to do with them, and someone else involved that was being held in the jail. Those women were extra loud and told stories about how prison differed from jail and how jail was a picnic compared to prison and the women there.

I was now sitting in an upright position listening to the stories and watching the ladies' interactions with one another. I was praying to hear them call my name and remove me from this scene, but that did not happen. Instead, I heard the Holy Spirit tell me to ask the women if they wanted to pray before they went before the judge. *What? Really, this is just too much,* I thought as I sat there pondering how I was going to do this. How could I interrupt these intense conversations? Should I stand when asking, stay by the wall or go to the center? I was having a pow-wow in my mind and ten minutes had easily passed since the directive was heard.

I made up my mind that I was going to do it, but I was certainly not happy about it. I took a deep breath and readied myself to get up. Just then, one of the women who came from prison spoke up loudly and said, "Listen, everyone, I want to say a prayer before we go to court so anyone who wants to can come join me in a circle." To my shock and surprise, everyone in the room got up and held hands, bowed their heads, and silently waited for prayer.

Tears streamed down my face. I had failed miserably and there was nothing I could say. God always has a ram in the bush and His will and work will be completed, if not by you or me then by another. Did I really think I was the only one who was incarcerated that loved the Lord, the only one who served Him?

Moments after the prayer was completed, the doors opened, and half of the women were called out. Minutes later the guard called my name and said my case had been rescheduled for a later date in two weeks. I would be going back to my tank. To say that my heart was crushed, and I felt defeated would be an understatement. Not because I did not see the judge, but because I had let my Heavenly Father down. I could not believe I was afraid and not willing to acknowledge Him, my Lord and my God, the lifter of my head, my Savior and Redeemer happily and openly in my life.

I was feeling confused and I wondered, *Am I only a Christian when it is convenient for me or when I want to witness to someone of my choosing or am I not truly a Christian at all?* I was devastated and ashamed, so I sat there like a wounded animal caught in a trap, hurt, bewildered, and dismayed.

I repented to God and asked Him to give me another opportunity to witness for Him. I knew with certainty in any other situation, me being fearful to share God, His Word, and His Salvation would never happen again. The mental pain I was experiencing was more than I ever expected or wanted to know. I went back to the tank, lay on the bed, prayed, and cried myself to sleep. My cellmates thought it was because I was not being released, little did they know those tears and sounds of sorrow were from a much deeper, agonizing realization. I was not as committed to sharing the Gospel as I believed.

Who knew that the shame I felt from that day would propel me in the days to come to study, pray and fast for boldness and strength for every assignment at every appointed hour…But God?

Humble yourselves therefore under the mighty hand of God, that He may exalt you in due time.

— 1st Peter 5:6 (KJV)

White Bar Soap

It has been eleven days now since being incarcerated and I have not had a bowel movement in all that time. I am sure it is because of the change in my dietary intake as well as stress. Regardless of what is causing the blockage, my stomach is aching something terrible and now I am gassy and smelling like sour milk. Is it too much for a sister to ask for a laxative around here?

It is five thirty in the morning and the guard is passing out the mail. I am sitting in the day room because I am expecting to receive some mail from my family and friends. Sure enough, when the female officer comes to my unit, my name is called. As she opens the two letters, she has for me and begins to inspect the contents, I quietly say to her. "Ma'am, I have been constipated for some time now, is there anything you can give me to help me eliminate?"

She looks at me with her forehead wrinkled and adamantly says, "No!"

"Well, then what am I supposed to do?" I ask.

She answers sarcastically, "Push hard and hope you don't get hemorrhoids."

Without hesitation I responded, "You have got to be kidding."

She sucked her dingy yellow teeth with the huge overbite, rolled her half-opened eyes as if terribly annoyed at my statement, and said, "Just fill out a request for medical." And with that, she called the next name.

Medical request, I have heard about that, but unless you were bleeding profusely, vomiting your guts out, or writhing in pain, your request usually has a ten- to fourteen-day waiting period, and that was way too long. I was already having discomfort sitting and I needed some relief. I walked back to my bunk, disappointed and dismayed as I prepared to read my mail.

Looking up at the ceiling, I whisper, "Jesus, I could use some help; I am not going to make it much longer in this state." Almost as soon as the plea for help left my lips, there was my answer standing in the doorway. Martha, one of the ladies that was waiting to see if she too would receive mail, was ear-hustling and overheard my conversation with the guard. Her face was flushed, and she was bent over laughing with her right hand extended with a bar of white soap in it. She hurled it at me and said, "Consider this a gift."

I looked at Martha and then over to Marissa, my roomie, who was sitting on the bottom bunk across from me reading. Marissa glanced at me and then over at the door. Looking at

Martha standing there with the soap, she then looked back at me and said, "Oh, you must need to doo-doo."

Wait, what the what! How in the world did she come to that conclusion? I was clueless, intrigued, and anxious all at the same time. Martha came in and confirmed she overheard my earlier conversation and that she had a tried, true, and proven remedy. Well, that was all I needed to hear. "Great," I said. "What is it? Where can I get it? And how fast will it come?"

Martha said, "Right here, right now. And it depends on how clogged you are." She threw the white bar of soap to me with purposeful aim.

"I don't get it," I said. "What's the punch line?" I was not amused, and the discomfort was making me irritated with all the silliness.

"No punch line, that bar of soap is your sure-fire enema," retorted Martha.

I must have had a look of sheer shock and disbelief on my face because both ladies looked at one another and fell over laughing. They thought it was so hilarious. Tears were streaming from their eyes. My cellmate Marissa composed herself and said, "You have to break off a chunk and shove it up your butt as far as you can."

As you might have guessed, they burst out with laughter once again. This loud display of chuckling, snorting, and shenanigans woke up our top bunkmate Diane, who slept over Marissa. Diane instantly rose and wanted to know what was so funny. The ladies had no problem explaining to her that my bowels were blocked, and I could not poop and was in pain.

I felt as embarrassed as that husband in those Metamucil commercials, which by the way I would have traded all my commissary for a dose of some of that stuff. Diane threw her two cents in, without anyone asking, and began to share her testimony of how a piece of the white bar soap gave her almost immediate relief and revolutionized her life.

I thought, *What do I have to lose? Well, except the obvious.* So, after rolling my eyes at all three of the women, I took the advertised phenomenon-working package and went to the doorless area where the commodes were. I broke off a piece of the white bar soap; the chunk was just big enough to test but small enough that it would not damage anything upon insertion. I used it and then I sat and waited for the miracle to begin.

Nothing happened. *Did I just get pranked by that group of women? Was this some sort of new-person initiation stunt?* I wondered, because it sure seemed like it. I was on my way to find out, and when they saw me coming they assured me that it would work. I just needed to be patient and give it some time. They also cautioned me that I should wait close by the toilets because when it was time, it would certainly come forth like a volcano and no amount of squeezing could stop that eruption.

Approximately eleven minutes after I started the experiment, I felt a rumbling in my stomach. Six minutes after that, bless the wonderful name of Jesus, I had a strong urge to move expeditiously in the direction of the crapper. *Eureka! Hallelujah!* Truly I can say, without doubt, I sang because I was happy, and I sang because I was free. *Glory be to God!*

I do not know why it surprised me so, I knew God would supply my every need no matter how big or small. I guess I just was not expecting it to happen so fast. This incident reminded me that He is always there working it out for me. Who knew He can and will use our every experience to teach a lesson that will draw us closer to Him? Who knew He could and would use even a small bar of white soap to work a miracle? Who knew...But God.

If you remain in me and my words remain in you, ask whatever you wish, and it will be done for you.

— John 15:7 (NIV)

They Called Me Church

Time was winding down and almost everyone was in the day room playing cards, doing hair, or chatting. I had just taken a shower and was now sitting on the bunk assigned to me, completing my hygiene care and trying to hurry before the guard came to do a count. When it was time for count, everyone had to line up in the day room, give their last name and spin number at the guard's command and immediately go into their cell to be locked down for the night.

I had three cellmates at that time, so every bed was accounted for. Those ladies were easygoing and of different ages and nationalities. All of them said they were Christians, and one stated she was Catholic but had not been inside a church since elementary school. They all wanted prayer before they went to sleep, and because they saw me reading my Bible and praying regularly, they asked if I would be the designated prayer person each night.

The walls were paper thin, but I did not mind at all. In fact, I enjoyed praying aloud every night. This night was different though. I asked for prayer requests as I usually did and began the prayer by giving thanks to God for His goodness and for who He is, I gave Him the requests and petitions that were given to me and I began to pray for the other women in the jail.

That is when things changed. The Holy Spirit took over the prayer and I began to pray in unknown tongues. I could feel the tears streaming down my face. After some moments in this prayer style, I could hear my cell mates joining in the prayer as well, with "Amen!" and "Yes, Lord!" or other words of agreement. During my time of praying in tongues, it sometimes switched, and I prayed in the natural.

Suddenly, I began binding and losing in my native tongue as led, and two of the things I bound were fornication and adultery in the jail. It was known that many women participated in this practice and there were several in the dorm. I prayed against stealing, fighting, court cases, drugs and whatever else I heard for at least fifteen minutes before the Holy Spirit released me. Once I finished, I fell on my bunk and cried for a while, giving thanks to GOD for answering our prayers.

The entire tank was as silent. It was as if someone were standing there with a weapon threatening anybody who made a sound. Approximately ten minutes later, as I was nearing unconsciousness, two women who were known sexual partners with one another and housed in the same cell, began to argue, cuss, and curse one another. They said all sorts of rude and hurtful comments to one another. This behavior must have continued for about five minutes before silence filled the place once again.

I slept-in the next morning because I was drained, and awoke around seven-thirty. When I was on my way to begin my daily hygiene care, I noticed that one of the ladies, April, who was having same sex relations and was in the disagreement the night before was in the day room while the other woman was gathering her belongings.

It turned out she, Gwenn, was packing because she pulled train earlier that morning, which meant she was about to be removed from jail and taken to prison. She was throwing things in her bag and fussing and cussing while preparing to leave. As I returned to my cell and sat on my bunk that I had previously made, Gwenn, the woman that was packing, took her stuff to the front of the cell block by the bars and asked very loudly, "Who was that praying last night?"

Another woman in the day room answered quickly, "That was Church."

"Who?" she asked.

My cellmate, as she was leaving the room, said, "It was Ms. Alicia, my roomie, and we call her Church."

After that response, Gwenn swiftly approached the door and entered where I was. "That was you praying?" she asked.

I responded that it was. Then she asked, "Who told you to pray for everybody in here? I did not ask you to pray for me or about any situation I was in, so what gave you the right?"

I looked her in her eyes and said, "The Holy Spirit gave me the right to pray for you and your situation because He loves you and wants the best for you."

Gwenn snapped and came in closer, "I get so tired of you holy rollers trying to force your beliefs and doctrines on everybody." She went on, "Pray for your own f-c--ng self, because if you keep putting your mouth on things that do not concern you, then you are going to find yourself in a situation you cannot get away from."

I could feel my flesh getting hot and I was ready to match her energy. I said, "I do not bow down to or back down from threats. I will continue to do as God instructs me to when He tells me to. If you have a problem with what I do, then that is on you."

Gwenn got loud and began to clap her hands, "female dog, (but she said the actual B-tch word), do you think this is a game?"

I could see this escalating quickly, so I rose off the bunk in preparation for a physical attack. Gwenn was in my cell, and she had nothing to lose at this point. She was on her way to prison for robbing a drug store for large amounts of pharmaceuticals. I would not get a case because Gwenn came to my quarters with the mess. Yes, I was a born-again believer, but I was nobody's punching bag, so if trouble was what she came looking for, she was soon going to find it in me. I was and still am a work in progress.

So, when Gwenn saw me rise off the bed, she says, "Oh I see you 'Church.' So, you think you are bad? You got up like you want to do something. What are you going do garden tool (h-e)?"

I did not say a word, I never was one for much talk when being confronted. Gwenn came yet closer and was now too close to my space for comfort. I told her, "Back up out of my face."

Some women were now sitting on the bench by the door, my roommates were sitting on their bunks watching and April, who had come in the room, was standing in the corner. She said, "This why nobody can deal with you now, Gwenn, because you are so obnoxious. Leave her alone."

That statement made Gwenn even angrier, if possible, she turned to April, "Oh, so you her guardian angel? You on her 'jock' now?" Gwenn turned back to me, saying, "So, you want to be like me on the low?" As she was speaking, she pushed me and in turn, I pushed her back and it moved her from the spot she was standing and out of my space.

Next thing you know, Gwenn punched me so hard in my jaw that my head almost spun around like that little girl in *The Exorcist.* Before the right scripture could enter my thoughts, my fist came from the deep south with a haymaker so strong it slammed into her face and threw her head backward like a bobblehead. The fight was on.

We both charged at one another with fists a-blazing. I tell you on that day, Matthew 5:39 was nowhere in my thoughts. I did not turn the other cheek, instead, I tried to beat the living hell out of her. I was past angry, and all the frustration I had was manifesting during that fight. It was an all-out brawl, punching, kicking, slapping, cussing, biting, and hair-yanking. It was fierce.

I could not even tell you why, but the ladies began pulling us apart and encouraging us to stop fighting. Never heard of that happening in jail or prison before. They were pulling me toward my bunk and her toward the door. In hindsight, that was the quietest fight ever. All that could be heard were the noises Gwenn and I were making. There was no screaming, no fight chants, no guards bursting in the tank…nothing. I think the ladies were in total confusion seeing that side of me. It was a far jump from me reading scriptures, encouraging the women, sharing commissary, and praying at night. Deep down, I knew all that was tarnished by the heated one-on-one fight.

I sat on my bunk for a moment while accessing my body, gathering my thoughts, and wrapping my mind around what just happened. My face was hurting as well as my head where my hair was almost pulled from the roots. I also had pain in my left thigh and a bite on my upper left arm, right above the crease in the front of my elbow. I could hear the women whispering about the situation as well as Gwenn still cussing about how I should have minded my own business.

My roommate asked if I needed anything and went on to say she knew Gwenn started it and how I had to defend myself. I looked at her and nodded and she smiled back and said, "I did not know you could throw hands like that, Ms. Alicia," then she left the room. Just like that, I was no longer being called Church.

I leaned back against the wall and imagined how the entire government of Heaven must have stared in shock at my behavior. The guilt, shame, regret, and condemnation that was flooding my mind was a whirlwind of taunting thoughts being hurled at me from what seemed all directions, but it was only me and the mental images I allowed to consume me. I was so embarrassed and thought, *What should I do? How am I going to come back from this one? How can I justify my behavior?*

My witness was blemished, I had allowed my flesh to override the knowledge I had of how a believer should behave. I could have prevented the situation if I had not been so carnal and ready to engage. I wondered, *Why was it so important to let everyone know I was no pushover? Were my true intentions to defend and protect myself or did I want the women to know I was not to be messed with just because I could pray in the spirit? Did I want them to know equally that my natural side was no joke?*

I had to evaluate my actions by the Holy Spirit, and what I discovered is…that which I thought I had been delivered from was lying dormant until the right situation arrived. The anger, rage, and confrontation demons surfaced, and I succumbed to them. I was better than I used to be, but still had a mighty long way to go.

I am not certain how long I sat there on that bunk, reliving the altercation. I was too ashamed to pray, so I just kept my eyes closed with my head leaning back against the wall. This position kept the women from coming in to talk with me, and I was thankful for that. I could hear my own breathing and it seemed to have gotten so dark and still. I could feel the tears roll down my face to my neck and rest on my chest. I was numb and I did not know what to do at this point, so I just stayed there in that position.

I snapped forward when I heard the guard yell Gwenn's name. She told her to say her goodbyes and that she would be back to get her in a few minutes. *Lord help me,* I remember thinking. *How can I make this right before she leaves?* I got up from the bunk and went to the door. The women who were in the dayroom were spread throughout the tank doing random things. I looked for Gwenn, but she was not out there, she was in her room with another lady who was giving her something on a piece of paper.

I walked over to the room Gwenn was in and asked if I could talk to her. She looked me up and down and went back to talking to the lady. I proceeded anyway, "Gwenn, I want to apologize for fighting with you. It did not have to come to that, and I am sorry that I let it happen that way. Would you please forgive me?"

Gwenn told me to go duck myself (but she used an f instead of a d). I again stated my sorrow for what happened and left her door.

Before going back to my room, I lifted my voice and addressed the women, "Excuse me, ladies, I would like to apologize for my behavior today. I am only human and sometimes my flesh gets the better of me. This is not an excuse, it is the truth." I went on to say, "God is not through with me, and I will make many mistakes on this Christian journey but that does not mean my walk is false, it only means I will continue to stumble, trip, and fall at times. Today is one of those times when my flesh side won momentarily over my spiritual side. I am trying my best and with the help of the Lord, I will continue to grow in His grace."

Some said they understood, they would have done the same, and that I did not need to apologize. Some said nothing, and one said she forgot I was a Christian the way I was swinging, and burst out in laughter.

I returned to my cell and sat on the bunk as I earnestly tried to understand how and why I reacted negatively so quickly. The day continued with normal occurrences: meals, games, talking, visiting other cells, and the count to turn in for the night. The guard never did come back for Gwenn as she said she would. I was dreading having to be locked in our cells that night because I did not feel worthy or absolved, even though I asked the Lord to exonerate me for my behavior.

I had not pardoned myself, and that was getting in the way of me wanting to lead prayer that night. I remember yawning and trying to turn in rapidly before the other women got comfortable on their bunks. It almost worked, but right before I could fall asleep, Gina, my cellmate asked, "Alicia are you ready for our prayer requests?"

You can only imagine how loudly I wanted to scream, "No, I will not be leading prayer! Somebody else do it." Instead, what I said was sure and took their prayers before the Lord. I ended with the Our Father prayer. That night's prayer was quick and to the point, I was even lying down as I prayed. Once done, I said good night, turned my back, covered my head, and lay still until I went to sleep. I desperately wanted that day to be over.

Early the next morning, while the doors were still closed, I heard the guard open one of the cells, and seconds later she yelled out for Gwenn. Gwenn answered, and the guard asked what her spin number was. Once Gwenn told her, she commanded Gwenn to get her things and follow her. The next thing I heard was the cell door closing moments before the bars to the unit slammed shut.

Nothing was the same in the unit for me after the fight—because I was not the same. I condemned myself for my actions and became my own roadblock. I did not know how to forgive myself or how to fight in the Spirit to regain my confidence and move forward from the ordeal I had allowed to consume me.

I should have gone back to reading the Bible in the dayroom, encouraging the women and all the other positive things I had done in the past. My focus should have been on those who did not know could see that believers make mistakes and fall short, but they get back up, ask for forgiveness, repent, and keep on going while working out their own soul salvation.

Instead, I walked with a defeated mentality which infected my entire being. Though I remained cordial, it was clear my light had dimmed. When I spoke with my family, I pretended I was good, just missing them and home.

I was transferred out of that unit and jail five or so days after the fight. I was moved to another county to address other charges against me, and I never spoke about that fight again. Until writing this book I had never revealed the fight situation. I settled in my mind that only those who were present with me in that jail, on that unit, would know what happened that day, and I did not plan on seeing any of them again. That fight was going to be a secret I would take to the grave, BUT GOD.

Why? Because I was ashamed that I acted so worldly. I reacted like I used to back when I was living life on the edge without regard for the consequences—before I accepted Jesus as Lord and Savior. Now I understand it was my foolish pride.

I wanted my family and friends to believe I was the bright beacon of light in the doomed and dark underworld. I worried what they would think and say if they knew I had taken off my self-placed halo and rolled around in the pit. So, I only shared things that would illuminate the viewpoint I wanted to portray, true but with a few omitted, yet pertinent, details.

However, with this book, the Holy Spirit had me revealing all the naked truths. So, I am spilling all the tea, and to be honest it is so liberating and refreshing. Hopefully, someone reading this has just been released from whatever bondage holding them captive as they try to hide embarrassing truths. Let God be glorified for every situation He has brought you through, brought you over, and brought you out of…regardless of what it was or is. God is able to turn everything around for His glory and your testimony.

Believe that your story will help others conquer and overcome, that exposing your vulnerability can encourage others to come forward sooner so they too can be set free. God is yet in control and because we belong to Him, He will see to it that _all_ things work together for our good. I imagine how the fight I had all those years ago will be able to set others free just by me sharing my story.

Our testimonies and truths show that our mistakes, downfalls, and shortcomings do not stop the plans God has for our lives. So, I encourage you to dust yourself off, get back up, and continue to press toward your mark. The good will be evident sooner or later at the appointed and ordained time, we just need to keep moving forward until then. As my mother used to say, God rest her soul, you will understand it better by and by.

Now I want you to know, brothers and sisters, that what has happened to me has actually served to advance the gospel.

— Philippians 1:12 (NIV)

Go Out Amongst Them

I was sitting on the bottom bunk rereading a letter that I had already answered, just to refresh my memory as I waited for the response to come. Mail call in jail is certainly a highlight for anyone on the receiving end, well, considering that it is not a dear John or other information of unwelcome news kind of letter. Nevertheless, I rose early every morning in the hopes I would have my name called to receive mail, and this day was no different.

My reading was interrupted by the still, small voice that you hear when the Holy Spirit speaks. He said for me to go out into the dayroom and read my letter and to take my things with me. The Holy Spirit told me to go and read in the big, near-empty dayroom on the hard, cold steel seats.

Not understanding why I had to do that, I gathered my letters, notepad, pictures, pens, and bible and proceeded into the dayroom. I sat at the first available table, which was located right outside of my cell room. I sat at the empty table and continued to read. I also looked through the pictures until I found one with the person I was about to write. A young woman came up and asked if she could borrow a few sheets of paper. I told her of course, and with that, she sat down and asked if she could borrow a pen as well.

She began by saying how she needed to write to her family and let them know where she was and how she was doing. She said she had not talked with her husband or her two children since a few weeks before she had come to jail. She was ashamed and did not know if they would even want to hear from her. She had been in jail for three months.

Shavana, the woman that was talking with me, was another one of the women that had been having relations with Gwenn. Gwenn was with Shavana before April arrived and took her place. Shavana said she was living that lifestyle while she was in jail because she did not have any finances and needed commissary, and she did not like being alone.

Shavana told me this only happened because Gwenn said she was going to take care of her and because she supplied her material needs. She figured it was the least she could do in return, but that she truly did not like it but it was a means to an end.

Shavana, who would now be the stud in any relationship that she would have in jail, wore her hair braided back in cornrows, she rolled the sleeves on her top up towards her shoulders, and her pants sagged off her behind revealing she wore boxers. Some evenings she would sport a sleeveless white t-shirt, whenever she hand-washed her top. She looked and carried herself like a male.

Nevertheless, she was ready to reach out to her family, and it brought tears streaming down her face when she talked about them. She wrote the letter, and I gave her a stamped envelope for it. She sent it off, saying she felt nervous but accomplished.

She asked questions about the Bible and God, and though I had not gotten my confidence back one hundred percent, I could not deny the love I felt by sharing God and His uncompromising Word with her. Shavana was present during the fight I had with Gwenn, but she believed I was true about my walk and representation as a born-again believer.

Shavana told me she had some ideas and information about Christ, but she never truly accepted Him into her life. She went to Sunday school and attended a Baptist Church when she was younger, but she did not have any type of relationship with the Lord in her adult life. She told me she and her husband would quarrel about this. He became saved during their marriage, and she did not, because she was not ready to give up her lifestyle. Shavana said she liked to drink, smoke weed, and club on a regular basis and that was driving a wedge between her and her husband.

Shavana was in jail because of a drunken hit-and-run accident she was in. Thankfully, the person she hit only sustained a broken shoulder and bruised ribs. She said she had been a fool and asked if it was too late for her; if she had missed the opportunity for Jesus to be her Savior because of her sins, especially those she committed while in jail. I smiled and told her absolutely not, that Jesus came to redeem her soul from every sin, just like He did and continues to do for me and everyone else who claims Him as their God.

Shavana's whole demeanor transformed, you could see her whole countenance change. She sat up straighter, lifted her head, made direct eye contact, unfolded her arms, and asked what she needed to do to become His child. *Hallelujah, Glory be to God!* I said, "Let me show you," and I opened the Bible to Romans 10. She read verses nine through eleven.

Once she was done reading, I asked her if she would allow me to take her through the sinner's prayer. She readily agreed, and with that, she was saved. I told her that her sins were forgiven according to the Word of God, she had a new slate, and her name was written in the Lambs' book of life. She cried and said if God would allow her husband to take her back once she got out in two months that would be the first thing she would tell him. Some of the others in the dayroom congratulated her and shared their testimonies with us, hugged her and we made it as special a day for her as we could.

Days after Shavana wrote to her husband, she received a letter back from him. When they called her name, she ran to the bars in excitement. This was the first piece of mail she had gotten since she had been there. She stood staring at the letter with tears streaming down her face as she shook her head and rocked from side to side. She clutched the letter to her chest and came and sat down at the first table outside my cell room. I smiled at her as she stared at the letter.

Because I did not receive any mail, I went back in my cell room, watching her while sitting on my bunk. Sometime later, after just staring at the letter and smelling it, Shavana removed the pictures and letter from the already opened envelope. She stared at the photos and tears began dropping on the table before a beautiful smile lit her face. Looking in my direction she asked if I wanted to see her family. Of course, I did. I got up quickly and went to join her in the dayroom.

Shavana showed me pictures of her two children sitting on top of a car eating ice cream, another of them and her husband in a pool splashing water, the third was of all four of them at a birthday party. The last one was of her husband standing behind her with his hands wrapped around her stomach as he leaned over her right shoulder.

Shavana was beyond excited, and she asked if I would stay as she read the letter. I did, and when she finished reading, she lunged at me and hugged me. "Alicia, they want to come to see me! "They want to come to see me today!" The day she received her letter was the same day the husband was coming for a visit. (In jail you do not get your mail the same day they receive it in the mail room, you usually get it three to five days later. So, the fact she was just finding this out was shocking but not surprising.)

Shavana began to panic because she wanted to see him desperately, but she did not want him to see her the way she was looking. Well, as you could imagine, word got around the cell quickly and women came forth with ways they could help get Shavana ready. We had makeup artists using fruit and candy for eyeshadow and lip gloss, hair stylists were taking out her braids, slicking back her hair and giving her a tease up in the front. Tailors were fixing her uniform, or at least giving her one that fit better. She got a new pair of socks and slippers to wear, one lady even let her use her good lotion.

When everyone was done, Shavana was ready to reunite with her family. She waited impatiently until the guard came to get her, which was six hours after she received the letter. We clapped and cheered her on as she walked nervously to the gate after being called out for her visit. She kept looking back at us for the encouragement, which we happily gave. When she got outside the bars, she did a happy wiggle dance and disappeared.

About an hour or so later, Shavana came back. She was radiant, glowing, and grinning. Her husband wanted her back, he missed her terribly and was extremely concerned when he did not know where she was. She talked about her children and how they missed her, how her husband kept telling her how beautiful she was, and how he could not wait to cook for her because of her obvious weight loss.

He also told her how much he loved her and wanted to care for her and that he would be back every weekend until the day he picked her up after her release. The icing on the cake was when she told him she had accepted Jesus as her Lord and Savior. She said he looked off and cried and then began to thank God for answering his prayers. He was overjoyed, which made her ecstatic.

I tell you when you obey the voice of the Lord, anything and everything can happen. Who would have guessed just by making myself available to the Holy Spirit's directives that day I would lead someone to Christ when that was not even my intention? I was busy trying to hide and heal from my own wounds and shortcomings. Furthermore, who would have known that sharing a piece of paper and a stamped envelope would be instrumental in bringing a family back together? Nobody, but God!

Brothers, if anyone is caught in any transgression, you who are spiritual should restore him in a spirit of gentleness. Keep watch on yourself, lest you too be tempted.

—Galatians 6:1

Bench Warrant

Weeks after being booked into the jail and finally getting into a daily routine, it was interrupted without notice by a guard shouting my name and telling me to pack my belongings. I was leaving. I had no idea what she was talking about, because I had not gone before the judge and a bail amount had not been set so that I could get out. Nevertheless, I gathered a few items and left the food and most everything else with my cellmates. I waited in the dayroom for the guard to come back for me and received all types of voluntary scenarios as to what was taking place, none of which made me feel good.

Thirty or so minutes after being summoned, the guard came back and escorted me and other women to a room where even more women were waiting. We were then light-stripped and searched, which means we were patted down and our mouths were checked. Then, we were taken down a freight elevator and put into different holding cells. It was at this point I was told I was not being released but that I had a bench warrant in another county and city and was awaiting the transfer team to come to get me and take me there.

Wait! What for? I wondered. Then reality hit me quick, fast and, in a hurry, *Oh yeah…probation violation. I'm going back to*

Anahuac. Seven years prior to this arrest, I was on a ten-year deferred adjudication for marijuana possession. I had not paid the court-mandated fines, which was enough of an offense, and now receiving this new charge was a direct violation of the terms of the probationary rules I was given.

This new charge happened from the time I was pregnant with my middle son and was receiving welfare. I took a private duty nursing case for a month and did not report my income, however, the accountant for the family I worked for did, so I was charged with theft. Both incidents were a violation of the judged-ordered conditions to remain free from incarceration, and therefore I had to return and face the consequences.

Even though the theft charge happened years before I was arrested and before I became saved and born again, it is with certainty that what is done in the dark will surface and come to the light. Shortly after being placed in the cell, the guard called for me. The constable was there, and I was about to be transferred.

The guard told me to hold out my arms, and when I did, she handcuffed me. She then took a large manila envelope and handed it to the male Caucasian officer, and signed a form that stated I was being released to his care for transport. The constable told me to follow him, and he opened the left back door of his squad car and told me to get in. Once I was seated, he closed the door and got into the driver's seat. It was only he and I in the smoked-filled vehicle, with a wired partition separating the front from the back. I remember being cold, nervous, and uncomfortable.

Once we got on the highway, the officer opened his window and lit another cigarette. The smoke he blew from his mouth was forced by the wind into the back where I was sitting. I sat all the way back and bent over with my head in my lap in an attempt to stop inhaling the smoke.

Once he finished smoking, he rolled up his window and turned the air conditioner up to freezing. I assumed the fetal position as best I could to keep warm. I stayed in that position for the duration of the fifty-minute ride. Once we arrived at the small station down an unpaved dusty road, I was taken out of the car by an awaiting female officer and escorted into an inside office.

Though this was a much smaller jail, the process was almost the same as before: receipt of property, fingerprinting, photo, changing into that facility's jail attire where I switched the orange for grey, and then being assigned to a cell and bed. I was given a square plastic container that held a toothbrush, bar of soap, washcloth, towel, deodorant, lotion, and a plastic comb. A trustee carried my plastic-covered thin mattress and a wool blanket that held a fitted sheet, a pillow, and a pillowcase rolled up in it and put it in the unit where I would stay.

Because the jail was small, the women's side housed two units. Each unit had five dorms, and each dorm had two private or one-person bedrooms. These private bedrooms were separated by a day room or common area. The common area had a stainless-steel bench and table attached to the wall to share, a mounted television to share, a private shower on each side of the room by the individual bedrooms, and a sink in the middle to share.

Each bedroom had a cement bed space hollowed in the wall where you placed your mattress, sheets, pillow, and blanket. There was also a table with a connected swivel seat, a sink, toilet, and mirror that were all stainless steel and the room was enclosed by bars. If they had a lockdown, you would go into your bedroom and the bars would close and lock. Each dorm could be and would be locked during lights out or bedtime without locking the individual room doors. In the day and evening time, you could leave your dorm and walk back and forth to other dorms in the unit.

When I arrived, the first unit was filled so I was placed in the second unit with the same setup. I was able to choose which room and bed I would take because the entire unit was empty. I was all alone. I choose the bottom bunk in the first room so I could at least hear some of the conversations from the other unit around the corner. I made the bed and settled in, and shortly thereafter fell asleep.

I was awakened early the next morning by one of the guards escorting a trustee who was bringing my breakfast. The hot topic of the day was the new girl, and that nw girl just happened to be me. The food at this small jail was much better than what they served at the county jail in Houston. The covered tray was filled with actual food that you could identify and enjoy. I was given scrambled eggs with two sausage patties, a muffin with butter, a banana, a carton of milk, and a carton of orange juice. Wow, that was certainly a great, unexpected improvement from the slop I had been served for the prior two weeks.

Shortly after breakfast, the guard came back with a trustee to retrieve the tray and told me she would be back to escort me outside for one hour of recreational time. This was another unexpected improvement and one that was certainly welcome. Once I reached the cemented rectangular enclosed area, I was surprised to see a basketball and a net that was attached to a flat metal slab hung on the wall, two tennis balls (no rackets), a few jump ropes, two frisbees, and a water fountain attached to the wall. The sun was shining brightly, and a cool breeze was blowing.

Again, I was alone; however, I decided to walk around the yard not only for exercise but also as an attempt to fully wake up, which did not happen. The time dragged on for what seemed like forever, and I was relieved when the guard came to check on me after about thirty minutes or so. I asked her if I could go back inside. She said she'd never had someone request to go back early, but she understood it could be a little boring being by myself. She said they had to keep the two units separated per policy.

Back to my own little corner in my own little world I went. What to do was the question at hand. I decided to write letters to my family and church family, which always made me feel better and passed the day along. I had only completed my first letter to my eldest son when the guard came by with the trustee and a filled mop bucket. It was mandatory that the dorm was cleaned daily. The water already had a solution in it, and there was also a broom with a dustpan, a cleaning towel and a bottle of cleaning mixture was also issued. I was told to leave all the supplies at the bars once I finished cleaning.

When they came back to pick up the bucket and other things, they brought a cart with my lunch tray. My first lunch consisted of two pieces of fried chicken, mashed potatoes with brown gravy, peas and carrots, a roll, iced tea, and a square piece of vanilla cake. To be honest, this was better than the lunches I had at home.

After lunch, I made some collect phone calls on the pay phone located in the unit and then proceeded to write my letters. I also filled out the commissary slip they had left on my lunch tray. Commissary days were once a week, but because I had just arrived I did not have to wait until the regular day and was allowed to order early. They had a wide variety of items on their three-page list, from food to clothing to snacks and hygiene care, and many things in between.

The money I'd brought with me was more than enough for the inexpensive items, so I took my time and ordered everything from stamps to peanut butter, socks, candies and a hairbrush. I was trying my hardest to adjust to my surroundings and prepare for the time I would have to do until I could go home.

I stayed at this small jail for two days before seeing the judge. When I went before him, I was shackled with my hands in front and there was a long chain that hung down and connected to the ankle cuffs. To my surprise, when I arrived at the courtroom most of my entire family and church family were there in support. Of course, seeing them brought instant tears that were uncontrollably streaming down my face, accompanied by many sniffs from my snot-dripping nose.

My mother, sons, pastor, and sister-in-love sat behind me, and my then-youngest son, Trenton (truth), who was two at that time pulled at my shirt and called out Mommy. My heart felt as if it leaped into my throat. As I turned toward him, Trenton reached out his arms for me to take him, but I could not raise my arms above my waist because I remained shackled the entire time. Even if I was not shackled, I do not believe they would have allowed me to hold him. Trenton began to pout and then began to cry. His big brother Durrell (truth) took him from my mother and patted his back and rocked him quietly until he was silent.

As my lawyer and the District Attorney presented their sides of the case, the judge decided enough information was not adequately presented and he reset the case for a later date. My lawyer said this was in my favor and I was instructed to get letters of support, along with family and friends' pictures that had me in them looking not only presentable but also wholesome. He said a letter of employment written out on business letterhead would also speak volumes. I was to have all letters sent to the judge prior to my next court date, which happened to be two weeks away.

Once I got back across the parking lot to the jail, I was instantly called for visits. I had over twenty people that wanted to talk with me and this small jail allowed every one of them the opportunity. Although they were no-contact visits, I could place my hand on the glass and simulate touching theirs.

My Trenton put his face up to the window and reached for my face. I blew him kisses through the screened wired vent covering and talked to him, which somewhat appeased him. My Durrell said he was looking out for him and when he got home, he would have his friends and Sunday school class write letters of support for me.

I teared up again hearing this and noticing how he had grown and matured in such a short amount of time. I remember being emotionally drained once I finished the visits, but also being overwhelmingly hopeful and encouraged by all the love, support, and positive conversations. I returned to the cell with confidence that this situation would be over soon.

Shortly after being back in the cell, I decided to take a nap. I knew my family and friends were returning home after the visit and I did not feel like writing a letter. Sometime during my nap, I felt this enormous force on my face. I had been asleep on my stomach with my head turned toward the wall, so the left side of my face was on the mattress. I slept with a pillow over my head to keep the light out of my eyes.

Something or someone was pressing the pillow down so that I could not breathe. I tried lifting my head but could not, no matter how I tried. Panic was setting in and I remember thinking I was going to die if I did not remove this pillow. *Jesus, help me! Please, Lord, do not let me die. Help me!* I cannot tell you if that was a thought or if it came out of my mouth, but what I can tell you is that Jesus sent me help. I heard the Holy Spirit clearly tell me to turn my head. Not try and lift it up, but simply turn it the other way, and when I did, the pressure lifted, and I was able to throw the pillow off my head.

What I saw next scared me to the point I was noticeably shaking; I began speaking in tongues as I sat up on the bunk and drew my body into a ball, as if trying to protect myself from danger. There was a force in the cell with me. It stood about ten feet tall and was dressed in an all-black oversized robe with an attached hoodie. Once I removed the pillow, it lifted itself off the bed and looked down at me as it began to back away.

When I began praying and calling on the name of Jesus, it turned and left out the cell towards the bars. Sometime later, I got up and checked to see if it was still there and there was no one and nothing in the entire dorm but me. I called my pastor later that evening and she said it was a demon spirit, probably the spirit of fear or the spirit of death. I was trembling as she spoke.

She told me not to be afraid because the Lord was with me, and to keep reading the Bible and praying. She said the victory was coming my way and the enemy was angry. I prayed myself to sleep that night and the demonic spirit did not return, at least not in that jail.

Two days after court, I was told to get my things together because I was being bench-warranted back to Houston for court and would finally go before the judge there. Just as I began to settle into this new routine, I was moving again. I would be going back to the overcrowding, long waits to be processed back into the jail, cold showers, horrible food…the list goes on without any positives.

I had to throw the items I had just purchased away because I was in the unit by myself; however, the unopened things I told the trustee she could keep or give them away, I did not care. I knew the procedures now, but it did not make it any easier. Handcuffs on, I was put in the back of the car again and the transport began. I was headed to the next leg of routines I would endure. Who knows why I could not just stay in this jail until everything was completed But God?

Oh Lord, I know that the path of [life of] a man is not in himself; it is not within [the limited ability of] man [even one at his best] to choose and direct his steps [in life].

—Jeremiah 10:23 (AMP)

Taz

Being bench-warranted back and forth from one city jail to the next was such a long and emotionally painful process. However, coming from the small Anahuac city jail to the overpopulated cramped Harris County city jail added another level of aggravation that you would have to literally experience to totally understand. Nevertheless, here I was, going through the transfer once again.

I knew I would be booked back in and placed in a holding cell where I would spend the next ten hours or so waiting for them to push me through to the next phase. That process was where I would have the two-minute or less cold shower and be given the orange uniform. This time, to my surprise, they had one that fit; it was even a bit too big, which was a huge win for me...the Lord was showing Himself mighty and strong.

From here I would be, escorted to my new temporary housing unit where I would stay until I went before the judge. By the time I made it to the floor and was assigned a cell, I was exhausted and wanted nothing more than to make my "bed" and go to sleep. When I arrived at this new housing cell around one in the morning, the ladies were asleep, and I was able to do just that.

When I woke later that day around seven, I was introduced to the other three ladies I would be sharing cell space with. I was given their names and a brief synopsis for everyone in the tank. One of the ladies in the cell I was staying in called herself Taz. When I asked her what her real name was, she stated that it was none of my concern and that when and if I wanted to talk with her to address her as Taz. I asked her why she called herself that, and just as I expected, she said the nickname was given to her because she acted like the Tasmanian devil cartoon character and would tear down and destroy anything and everything that got in her way. She laughed as she said it, because I believe she thought this was a good thing.

"Well," I stated, "I will not be calling you any name that is attached to destruction and/or the devil."

She said, "Then I guess you and I will have nothing to say to one another," and with that, she exited into the dayroom.

Not again, I thought. What now? *How do I keep finding myself in the middle of these toxic interactions?* I found out from another cellmate that "Taz" was in jail for attempted murder, although she was claiming self-defense. She was no taller than five foot three inches but had a muscular build and I heard she was not to be played with. I was told she had a noticeably short fuse whenever she was threatened or crossed. That was both an introduction and a warning for me at the same time.

"Taz" and I were cordial with one another. We spoke every morning and said good night at the end of each day. We often sat at the same table and laughed at some of the same things. We even had great dialogue, all without me calling her by that demonic nickname.

It was on day five, I believe or somewhere around that time, when my name was called to receive mail. I was not expecting any, but was overjoyed to receive whenever it came. It was also on that day that "Taz's" name was called to receive mail as well. She was already in the dayroom, so she more than likely knew mail was coming for her because I do not recall her normally being up early like that.

The only thing with receiving mail in jail was they do not call you by any nickname regardless of who you thought you were or what status you attempted to hold. Receiving mail is one of the rare times they call you by your government name, and they called her name loud and proud. She looked around, and there I was looking right in her direction with a smile on my face that must have pierced her very existence because she took her mail and stared at me until she retreated into her cell and back to her bunk.

I am certain she was crushed because she turned her back to the door and did not even open her envelope. She stayed in the cell room most of the day, coming out only to go to the restroom, shower, and to get her food. She was extremely quiet that whole day, as if her entire world had just unraveled.

I did not bother her and neither did anyone else for that matter. It is an understood, unspoken rule in jail that when someone has their face turned toward the wall you should leave them alone. The morning turned into noon, noon into evening, and evening into night without incident. The normal day-to-day activities came and went with no new issues arising or any new residents entering.

I remember praying that night for the entire tank, for court appearances, for the judges to be lenient, I prayed for our families, and for wisdom. I then drifted off to sleep and slept well the entire night and deep into the next morning. I didn't wake until around eight, which is late in jail since the morning activities begin at five o'clock.

After completing morning hygiene and getting something to eat; I had long missed breakfast. So, it was the commissary stash for me. I decided to talk with "Taz" who had entered the cell and was sitting on her bunk staring at me. Talk about the elephant in the room! I began with, "So, are we going to address this or are we going to pretend like it never happened, Mildred?"

Whoa, me calling her by her first name almost got my head ripped off. She jumped up from the bunk, grabbed her head, spun around, and got low and in my face. She said with clenched teeth, "You better act like you never heard that name, you understand? I do not want to hurt you, but I promise if you say that name again I will take you out."

I stared at her, and to tell you the truth, fear tried to creep in. I asked her, "Do you truly want to hurt me just because I know your true name? I do not understand, because I like it. It is kind of cute and fits you."

She acted like I had not said a word. She hit her fist in her other hand and said. "That name is a joke. It has nothing to do with who I really am, and nobody ever addresses me by that name…ever. Mildred went on to say, "Taz is my name. My twin sister 'Blade' gave it to me right before we both got jumped into their gang family. Taz was the name that gave me power and balance so I could gain credibility and respect."

Mildred said her sister, who was four minutes older than her, told her that if anyone ever came against her that she should not stop fighting until she could no longer move. Mildred was told to use anything and everything in her pathway to make sure she would come out victorious, and by her own admission, that is exactly what she did from the age of fifteen until the day she was arrested.

Blade (whose government name was never discussed) was given that name because she was deadly with a switchblade, her weapon of choice. I was told that she was extremely crafty, conniving, and manipulative and would be up on you before you knew she was coming.

Blade was the one who had decided she and Mildred needed to join the gang so they could have their basic needs met once their crack-addicted mother went to prison. I got the impression that whatever Blade wanted, she usually got especially when it came to Mildred.

For years, they moved higher and higher up the ladder in the gang and they were unstoppable according to Mildred. They had it all, respect from their peers whom they considered family, money, a place to live, each other, and way more power than they could have ever imagined.

Mildred said things were better than they ever expected, until the impossible happened. The gang they were in got ambushed one evening and their leader was murdered in the process of the all-out fight. Two other members were badly injured and did not make it through surgery and the morgue was their destination on that night. What seemed like the indestructible family unit the twins had come to enjoy and depend on, had begun to crumble right before their very eyes in a moment's time.

Just like you would see in the movies, their first plan of action was revenge. Everyone agreed they had to regroup, get strapped (with guns and weaponry), and avenge their leader and sisters' deaths. I was told two days later, they went on the hunt. When I inquired if they found the people they were looking for, Mildred smiled, winked, and said, "I do not know what you are talking about." With that she laid back on the cot and closed her eyes as if she were reminiscing or replaying the entire scenario in her head.

That moment of satisfaction was short-lived for Mildred however. She suddenly sat up, looked around and asked, "Can you believe my own f-c--ng sister tried to kill me?" Then she asked me to excuse her language, regardless, the expletives continued throughout her story.

Turns out Blade wanted to be the new leader of the gang, but because of her selfish and uncontrollable ways, other members wanted Mildred to assume the position. Both twins were interested, but Mildred wanted more of a family unit, a place where the team could feel safe and loved. Blade wanted to be revered by other gangs and members of her own group, and she wanted everyone to know she did not tolerate any foolishness or there would be penalties and repercussions for anyone who attempted to cross her or her leadership.

Because the gang was conflicted as to who should lead, there had to be a showdown. Usually, this would consist of a fight until one person surrendered to the other, but because Blade knew she could not beat Mildred, she secretly produced an idea prior to the battle to ambush Mildred and kill her. When I heard this, I exclaimed, while holding my chest, "Mildred, I know you are lying!"

Mildred made this growling noise and said, "I warned you not to call me by that name."

I apologized, and added, "So what should I call you, because as I said, I will not be calling you any name attached to the devil." We agreed an acceptable name would be Ms. T, and with that, we moved on to the murder plot.

Blade's plan was for her and two of her closest allies in the group/gang/family, was to go on an outing with Mildred and get her high and drunk, and then hold her down so Blade could easily kill her. However, Blade was acting extra nervous, and she did not want to smoke or drink which never happened before according to Mildred. She kept falling back in the rear instead of trying to lead the group up front, which was her normal custom. Mildred said she felt uneasy and knew something was not right, although she could not have imagined what was planned.

The two females attempted to grab Mildred, but if you could see her physique, you would know and understand that was not an easy feat. Mildred, by her own account, put a hurting on both and managed to get the switchblade away from her sister in the process of the fight. Although Mildred was aware her own twin sister was trying to kill her, she said she threw the weapon and proceeded to whoop her sister as if she were her enemy instead of her twin sister.

Mildred dropped her head as she was retelling this part of the story, and I could see the tears sliding down her face and gathering at her chin. She looked up at me, and as she wiped at the tears, she said with a now rigid face and forceful voice, "I am in this world all alone now, so whatever happens when I get out, I do not care. It is eat or be eaten in these streets. Nothing can be worse than your own twin attempting to murder you for a position, which I would have willingly stepped aside from and let her have. I would have been her biggest supporter, just like I have always been." With that, she slid back on her bunk, pulled her knees up to her chest, and exhaled.

I rose off the bunk where I was sitting and moved across the room to where she was. I sat on the side of the bunk and looked at her for a while. "What?" she snarled. "Why are you staring at me like that? I knew I should have not told you any of that. I should have kept to myself like I always do. I need to realize it is only me, and I must live like that and not let nobody get close to me ever again. That is the way I will make it, and is how I am going to survive and move ahead."

Although I was hearing what she was saying, I knew it was out of hurt, abandonment, and betrayal that she was speaking. I knew Ms. T needed love and I knew the One who could give it to her. I said, "You are not alone and you do not have to ever be alone again."

She said, "You signing up to be my friend?"

I told her I could be, but that I knew someone that would always be there for her even when I could not, and that He would always help her make it through. She looked at me intently but said not a word. "Jesus," I said, to which she sucked her teeth and proceeded to get up from the bunk.

I grabbed her arm and asked her to wait. "I knew you were going to sneak religion in somewhere," she said, "I just did not know when or how you were going to ooze it into this conversation."

"I am not talking to you about religion," I stated. "I want to talk with you about a relationship, the greatest one you will ever have in your life."

"Just go ahead and say what you need to say, but I should tell you that you are wasting your time," she said, while sitting back and turning her whole body toward me. She looked at me intensely yet sarcastically and seemed to be eager for the talk to be over.

"Well, for starters," I said, "Jesus loves you just as you are, and there is nothing you can do to ever stop Him from loving you. He will never turn His back on you. Ms. T, all you must do is invite Him into your life. Do you believe that Jesus is the Son of the Living God?

She said, "Yeah, I heard that when I used to go to Sunday school back when I was living in a group home." She went on to say that she asked Jesus to be her personal Lord and Savior back then and she was even pushed down into the water as part of a big ceremony.

"Oh, you got baptized as well, that is so amazing. What changed that you stopped going to church?"

"Life," she said. "My sister and I ran away from the group home. Those folks were pretenders and were only after the check. Being on the streets is different from being anywhere else, you need food, shelter, and money. You want to do good, and you try to do good, but you quickly learn to go with the flow and the flow out there in those streets is get with it or get got. So, we did what we had to do to survive and that had nothing to do with church or God."

"I understand that, truly I do, but you are here now, and you have an opportunity to change things and leave here with a new purpose and new goal."

Ms. T looked at me for a while and smiled. She said, "Alicia, when I leave here, I am going back to the streets. I am going back to the life I had before I came here. My self-defense claim will stick, and the other small charges will be dismissed with time served. This little time I am here will give me time to plan and create my revenge because vengeance will certainly be mine. Once I leave here, I am going back with one purpose in mind.

"You ready for this?" she asked as she leaned forward. "My intention is to cripple my sister to the point where she is severely suffering and just short of death. I want her to know and understand she caused me to treat her like the betrayer she is, then you know what I am going to do?" she asked.

"No," I answered, because I truly did not, but was anxiously awaiting her response.

Ms. T went on to say, "I and the rest of the crew are going to take care of her for the rest of her life. Why? Because she is my blood and my family."

After the utter shock subsided, I was about to begin talking, gearing up to give additional points about forgiveness when she cut me off.

"Alicia you cannot save everybody. You did your part, you shared Jesus and His love and forgiveness with me, and I know that and believe that. Now, I must choose to follow or not, it is up to me from here on out. So, relax and leave it alone. I respect your dedication to help bring change and you did what you needed to do and that's all you can do." She got up and walked toward the door, "You do you, ladybug, because I swear I will do me when I leave."

I said, "Ms. T, you know I will keep praying for you."

She looked back and said, "Would not expect anything less from you," she winked and left the room and we never spoke about the situation again.

I am not certain what happened with Ms. T, if she fulfilled the intent of her heart or if Divine intervention prevented her and she turned from her wicked ways. Who can turn someone's heart when they are passionately prepared to get revenge or die trying...nobody But God!

I planted the seed, Apollos watered it, but God has been making it grow. So neither the one who plants nor the one who waters is anything, but only God, who makes things grow.

— 1st Corinthians 3:6 (NIV)

Face to Face Warfare

It was unusually hot this morning and I had sweated most of the night, so I arose as soon as the bars opened and went to take a shower in an attempt to cool off. The early morning water helped some, but I knew from the loud hum of the massive fans in the main hallways that the day was going to be heated in more ways than one.

I had stopped at the first table by the showers to dry my wet shower shoes and put my things in order, when I noticed Vanessa, a nineteen year old youngster, standing in the doorway. She had arrived four days prior and the buzz was that she was in jail because she deeply sliced her much older married male lover while attempting to cut off his penis. She had done so because he did not want to pull out while they were having intercourse and instead tried to get her pregnant, which she did not want to happen.

Her male friend had not called the police, her neighbors did when they heard him screaming. They then stated they saw him covered in blood running from Vanessa's apartment with his clothes in his hands. Upon investigating, the police found out he was at Vanessa's place and she was arrested. Her lover, Robert, had come and put money on her books, visited her, and told her he loved her and would be there for her. The jailhouse lawyers told Vanessa she would have to do state jail time because it was an aggravated offense.

Once I finished with my things, I arose and headed to put them in the room. Vanessa said hello and asked if I had some paper she could use. I told her I did and for her to give me a moment. Once I put my hygiene things away, I returned to the dayroom with the paper and a magazine.

Vanessa had moved to a table closer to where my room was and was tapping on the table while sitting on her knees and moving her head as if she were hearing music playing. I walked over and handed her the paper and she thanked me. She asked if she could ask me something, and I said sure. She wanted to know if her married lover did not want to press charges would she be released? I honestly did not know. All of this was new to me, and I told her just that. Almost instantly, Charisma, a light-skinned, big-eyed, loud-mouthed woman of around twenty-six came over and joined in the conversation as if she had been invited.

Charisma said of course they would unless the state picked up the charges. If that happened, it would not matter if Robert did not want to press charges, the charges would stand regardless. This made Vanessa physically nervous. "How will I know?" she asked. Charisma told her she would find out when she went to court.

Vanessa stated she had talked to Robert, and he said he told the police he was trying to cut some fruit when the knife slipped and he sliced himself. The police did not believe him, but Robert assured them that was the truth, and he was not going to say otherwise or press charges on someone who did nothing wrong.

Charisma then went on to say how lucky she was and how Vanessa should know Robert, the married man, is her soul mate and they were meant to be together.

I blurted out, "That is insane! Robert is married and cheating on his wife with Vanessa." I continued, saying, "Willingly having a child with him would not be wise. If he is not faithful to the woman he married and took a vow to, why would you expect him to be faithful to you? Neither of you deserve the disrespect of how this man used both of you for his pleasure and selfish desires.

"God would not give you another woman's husband. You deserve better than what you are accepting. Why do you not want your own man?"

She said she did not know, but that Robert was kind and took care of her and her needs and she thought that was enough for her. Charisma burst in that it was more than enough and that if Robert was doing all those things for her then he genuinely loved her. She then asked to see Vanessas' hand. She took her hand and began to look at it, I watched silently, anticipating what was about to happen, and I was correct.

Charisma began rubbing Vanessa's palm as she closed her eyes and moved her head around in circles before leaning it backward and exhaling with a loud sigh. I was pleading the blood of Jesus in my mind because I knew what was coming would not be good. As Charisma regained her composure, she stated that she just had a visitor who told her that Vanessa was supposed to have twins with Robert. She went on to say that this married man was her soul mate, and they would soon be together forever because the wife would suffer an unexpected departure. She also said that she could trust Robert with her life to do the right thing.

Before she could complete the statement, altogether righteous indignation rose inside of me, *How dare this woman tell a teenager that her future was being with a married man and bearing him children? The man is married for goodness' sake and is not only cheating on his wife as if that were not bad enough, but he was also having unprotected sex and attempting to get his much younger sidepiece pregnant.*

I looked Charisma dead in her eyes and said, "You have a lying spirit and what you just spoke was from the pits of hell." I proceeded to turn and look at Vanessa and told her, "What you just heard did not line up with the will or words of God. God would not give you someone else's husband. You are committing fornication and he is committing adultery and it goes against the teachings of God. This married man is using you and you should leave him alone."

Charisma blurted out that I was lying because I did not have the gift of a third eye so I could not possibly see what was going to happen in the future, but she could.

I told her, "I do not need a third eye, because I have the Holy Spirit living within me; the Spirit of Truth and of Wisdom. What Charisma was saying was going against the knowledge of God and was not accurate and I was going to stand in the gap and pull down that high thing that came to exalt itself above God's knowledge."

Charisma was beyond angry, she began saying I was jealous, that I was a liar, and that my punishment for coming against the oracles of the visitant would result in my demise.

"The Blood of Jesus is against that statement," I told Charisma. "You nor that with whom you take your orders from does not have the power to execute a demise over me. I am covered in the Blood of the Lamb and no weapon formed against me will prosper."

Charisma grabbed her head and shook it vehemently before rising and stating that I would not survive the night. She then began chanting something as she made her way back to her room.

Vanessa just looked on quietly with her eyes wide-open. She said that she was afraid for me and did not want to cause me death and that she would obey the visitant in Charisma's trance so that I would be spared.

I told Vanessa, "Stand still and see the power of God. Nothing was going to happen to me. I told her to believe the outcome and follow after the one who proved to show themselves mighty and strong in this situation."

We talked a while longer, and as I got up to go into the cell where I bunked, I could hear Charisma loudly chanting. She then began calling for justice to be served to the unbeliever. I continued on my way because one thing I knew for sure was that any weapon that was forming against me would certainly not prosper, in that I was confident.

I went about the day and evening as usual, casually passing the time with whatever small thing I could accomplish. Nighttime came and we completed the routine of being counted and locked in our small group cells. I prayed and went to sleep, same as before, nothing new, and I slept well.

For some reason I slept-in the next morning. I guess my body was tired and needed the rest. When I finally arose, Charisma was out in the day room talking loudly about how she was not to be played with, and that she had supernatural powers... ones that she did not like to use but that she had at her disposal when needed.

It was at this point that I exited the cell. I was on my way to begin my hygiene care when silence fell upon the open room.

Everyone sitting with Charisma turned their attention to me as I was walking toward them.

Vanessa jumped up from where she was perched and came and hugged me. I just looked at her and smiled. I did not want to say anything to her because I had not yet brushed my teeth and my breath was hot. She exclaimed loudly, "You lived, Alicia! You are alive!" and she hugged me again.

Charisma, now standing and staring in my direction, watched me walking with Vanessa toward where she was. Then she suddenly dropped her head and hurriedly went into the cell where she was being housed.

I continued on my way, and as I passed, the ladies began questioning and making fun of Charisma as she moved toward her cell room. They were saying things just loud enough to make sure she heard them. By the time I was finished with my care, things had almost gone back to some form of normalcy.

I was sitting on the bunk when Charisma and Vanessa approached the door. Vanessa wanted me to know that she was going to stop seeing Robert once she was released but that she would play the game until she got out to make sure he did not change his mind and squeal on her for attempted assault. She went on to say, "I do not know if I will be turning all Christian and everything, but I will go to church with my grandmother every now and again." She thanked me for the sound advice and left quickly before I could even get a word out.

Charisma, who was standing there looking at the floor, asked if she could talk with me, and I said yes, she could. I was inwardly rolling my eyes and feeling quite accomplished. Charisma went on to explain she did not want to harm me. However, since she was a young girl, she had been taught by her female family members, who were a group of practicing witches, sorcerers, and charmers that if someone tried to come against her words or chanting they must be made an example. Those who challenged them would have harm or death as their punishment.

She went on to say that she always hated those meetings and the sacrifices that would happen at them and what sometimes happened to her, but that was how she was raised. She then asked the most important question of her life, "Will the God you serve forgive me and will He be my God even after all the damage and harm I either caused myself or had been a willing participant in making happen?"

I looked her in her teary eyes, stood and walked towards her. I told her, "Absolutely NOT!" *Wait, what? Did I just turn someone away from repentance and accepting Jesus as their Lord and Savior?* Yes, my self-righteous self had decided this soul that was clearly crying out for redemption had done too much to be forgiven.

Charisma looked shocked and devastated as she went on to apologize for what she had attempted to do the night before. I stopped her and told her she should apologize to herself for thinking her witchcraft was any match for me. Not God, not the Holy Spirit dwelling on the inside of me, not even the angels God had given charge over me to watch and fight on my behalf. Nope, I was insulted that she and all that was operating inside her had the audacity to try to come against me. The pride that was in operation within me was appalling.

Charisma said, "Sorry. I won't bother you again."

I sat back down and glanced over at her with a look on my face that screamed that being sorry and leaving was wise. She turned around, put her head down, and left the doorway. I sat on the bunk feeling justified and vindicated because, after all, I had overcome a death threat.

Suddenly, I felt a presence whose strength I could never imagine. I was not scared, but I was instantly ashamed. It felt like the words I had previously spoken were choking me. I began trembling because I suddenly became aware of what I had just done. I became cognizant of the pride and foolish self-righteousness that was in operation within me and I wanted to be forgiven, cleansed, and restored. I wanted mercy; the kind of mercy Charisma was seeking but I refused to extend by not introducing her to the One who gives to all who seek.

I humbly asked God to forgive me and allow me to make it right. I prayed for wisdom and favor so that when I approached Charisma, she would receive me and what I had to say. I read scripture after scripture after scripture, and hours later, I gathered myself together, stood up, and went out into the dayroom. As soon as I made it to the first table, a guard approached the bars and opened them. She called Charisma and another lady's name and told them to gather their things immediately.

As I made my way towards Charisma's, room the guard stopped me and said there was no time for small talk because the women needed to come quickly and everyone needed to get back. Charisma came through the door with her stuff in her arms and headed toward the bars. The other lady was already there. The guard unlocked the gate to the bars, and they prepared to exit into the hallway.

I yelled out to Charisma, "I was wrong! Jesus loves you and wants you as His own. She looked back with confusion on her face, turned the corner, and walked out of my sight. I just stood there, with the other women looking at me. *I didn't do enough,* I thought. *I did not take her through the sinner's prayer, and I did not offer her the gift of salvation.* I felt so defeated, so useless, and so ashamed that my walk did not match my talk. I felt that I had secured Charisma's fate in eternal hell because she was a practicing witch. I was sick to my stomach and went back into the cell and slumped on the bed.

I desperately wanted this day that had barely begun to be over. I lay down facing the wall until I went to sleep. When I awoke, I stayed in the cell on my bed the entire day.

Who knows why Charisma was transferred out of the unit so fast and unexpectedly? Why was I not allowed to make amends and lead Charisma to Christ? This lesson was one I would *never* forget. Anytime anyone anywhere asks if Jesus would forgive them for their sins and be their God, I will most assuredly tell them, "Yes He will!" and lead them to His throne of Grace and salvation right then and there.

I was crushed in my soul, humbled in my spirit, and determined to extend the gift of God's love through Christ Jesus. I learned that day the real warfare was not from without but instead from within. Who knew evil could be in operation while openly and honestly trying to stand on and in the Word? But God, He alone knows how to get out of us what does not belong to Him.

Do not think you are better than you really are. Be honest in your evaluation of yourselves, measuring yourselves by the faith God has given us.

—Romans 12:3 (NLT)

Do not be overly righteous, and do not make yourself too wise. Why should you destroy yourself?

Ecclesiastes 7:16 (NIV)

Ms. Gertie's Blues

She came in after count once we were already locked in our cells for the night, so no one except for the other three ladies she would be rooming with saw her and knew anything about her when morning came. A new person meant new stories. For the rest of us it was like an adventure to find out their business and to what brought them to jail. From there, the jail house "lawyers" would determine their best plea, what they should say, what amount of time they would be given, if they should try and bond out or sit their time, and if they needed a free world attorney or if a court appointed attorney would suffice.

The day room would be filled early with those eager to get first crack at the new person. As soon as the doors were unlocked, the jail house lawyers would be the first out of the cells, their mission was in operation, full speed ahead. It was as if the one who got the information first would win something. So, like hungry lions, they were ready to pounce. This time was no different, and by the time I woke, before even exiting my bed I had the whole tea...

every juicy detail, plus some added adjectives and descriptions to make the new lady's story more interesting.

The new woman, Gertrude or Ms. Gertie as we came to call her, was 79 years old. She had been arrested and booked into jail because she helped her son, her only son and only child, get a rental car. She put her name on the lease and the contract, then made him a driver. Mind you, he himself was a grown man... child.

He took possession of the vehicle to travel with his female friend out of state for four days. They were going to New Orleans from Texas, and it should not have been a problem...it had not been before. This time was different, there was an issue, a major dilemma.

This time, Ms. Gertie's son decided to not return the car as he promised her he would. He also had the nerve, the boldness, the impertinence to lie and tell her he had dropped the car off early. So, when Ms. Gertie received constant calls from the rental company about the vehicle not being returned and being three days past due, she was surprised and was certain they were making a mistake.

She tried calling her son several times but to no avail. Her son even changed his number after a couple of days so she had no way to reach him. He and his much younger girlfriend seemed to have disappeared into the sunset.

It was that very act of defiance and thievery from her son that led Ms. Gertie to jail. She did not know the whereabouts of the vehicle she had signed for, nor did she have the money to pay for it any longer. Because she was the main renter, it was her responsibility, not her son's.

So, Ms. Gertie was taken to court, sued, and sentenced to jail for felony theft. This left her sister, niece, and nephew to further the investigation to try and find Ms. Gertie's son and the missing vehicle.

Ms. Gertie was a plump woman with round eyeglasses and silver hair that was pulled back from her face and hung past her shoulders. She was sitting up straight with her hands folded in front as one of the younger women offering her moral support twisted her hair and put it in a bun. She genuinely believed the ladies were able to give her insight and valuable information that she could share with her hired lawyer.

She was clearly naïve to the ways of the justice system and was holding on and clinging to any ray of hope her fellow inmates were offering up willingly, right or wrong. All day, as with any newbie, the ladies were very attentive and made sure she knew all the ropes…from what time chow would be served to which shower got the hottest to which guards you could expect what from. Everyone was usually very friendly with the newbies on their first day.

Day two, however, had a whole other outcome, one that would identify the reality of where you really were. This second day was the real first day for someone coming to jail. It was the day you knew without doubt you were locked up and that you were no longer in control of your life, let alone your desires or needs. On this day, conversations were not readily received, chore assignments were dictated, chow or commissary was not shared, and you had to personally decide how you were going to spend your days of lockup.

Each dorm was responsible for cleaning their own four-person quarters each day. The cleaning of the day room, shower, and commode area, along with emptying the trash, rotated weekly through the entire eight tank unit. On your dorm's week, every day the four women in your cell had to sweep, mop, empty trash, clean and sanitize the steel tables and benches, as well as the toilets and showers. This all had to be completed before noon. The guard would bring the cleaning supplies early in the morning— between 5 and 6 a.m. Supplies included a mop bucket with water and solution, a broom, a spray bottle with solution, two cleaning towels, a scrub brush and two large trash bags.

Once the chores were done, you placed the supplies back in the inner main bars for pick-up. Whichever dorm was overseeing cleaning the main living quarters was responsible for the care and return of the items.

On day three of Ms. Gertie's stay, her dorm was responsible for cleaning the main living areas. The females in Ms. Gertie's cell agreed that this seventy-nine-year-old, silver-haired woman who walked with a limp should have the chore of mopping the entire unit. The other oldest cellmate in Ms. Gertie's cell was thirty-two, and she was the one who handed out the cleaning assignments. While this soft-spoken mother whom anyone could see did not belong in the county jail, pushed the oversized yellow mop bucket out the inner bars with the mop still in the pre-made cleaning solution, the much younger women went about doing their menial labor as if nothing was wrong with their decision.

I got out of the shower, and while I was on the way to my cell to replace my hygiene items, I saw Ms. Gertie attempting to wring the water out of the mop. She was having trouble pulling the lever down far enough and hard enough to extract the excess liquid. I placed my things on the table and went over to assist her. She thanked me and grabbed for the mop to begin mopping the dirty, sticky floor.

I politely stopped her and grabbed the mop handle. I told her she did not have to do it; I would do it for her. Another young lady, Pina, said she would help as well, and another two who were sitting in the day room said they would help too. None of us wanted to allow this senior citizen to complete this physically challenging chore.

Ms. Gertie looked up toward the lights and smiled while shaking her head. She said, "I knew You would show Yourself mighty and strong." I knew she was having a conversation with our Father, the One who will never leave us or forsake us no matter where we end up.

Pina, who was of Latin descent, spoke Spanish with tears streaming from her eyes as she mopped. A Hispanic lady sitting with Ms. Gertie and I said Pina was having a tough time believing how little respect Ms. Gertie was receiving. She said that in their culture, seniors were honored, and that she would never allow someone Ms. Gertie's age to be mistreated. Pina stood about 4'10" and weighed around 105 pounds. She had a foul mouth and a short temper, and had been arrested for domestic violence. She stabbed her live-in boyfriend with a beer bottle for stopping her from beating her friend who made a pass at him while intoxicated.

After we mopped the entire unit, Pina and a few other women along with myself decided Ms. Gertie would not have to do chores as long as she was there because we would rotate and do her assignment for her. Not everyone agreed and the argument was that she was in the same predicament as everyone else and she should not expect any special treatment. That was their opinion though it differed strongly from ours, we did exactly what we said until the day Ms. Gertie made bail. We made it our duty to make sure Ms. Gertie would be taken care of to the best of our ability, with Pina leading the way.

It became evident that Ms. Gertie and Pina were becoming friends and forming a great bond. Each would eagerly and readily help the other with whatever they lacked. Pina moved into the cell with Ms. Gertie, and you could hear and see them laughing and sharing foods, doing hair, exercising and making the days more enjoyable for each other.

Pina was extremely protective of her new best friend and absolutely no one bothered or questioned the elderly woman in any type of negative way. It was a known fact that Pina was not wrapped too tight, and something would certainly happen whether she won or not…she would not give up until she was satisfied.

On a Thursday afternoon Ms. Gertie was called out because there was someone there to see her. She had been there six days by now and this would be her first visit. She was so excited. When the guard came to retrieve her, she promised Pina she would tell her everything when she returned.

Ms. Gertie was gone approximately two hours, in jail you move when they come for you, not when you want. Once Ms. Gertie came back to the unit, Pina was smiling and waiting to hear everything about the visit. It was a treat to hear about someone's visit or other information about their trip out of the unit. The news was great for Ms. Gertie, but bittersweet for Pina.

The visit was from Ms. Gertie's sister who informed her they got her a lawyer and he would be visiting her on Friday, the next day. She went on to say that once she went to court and bond was set, then she would be able to leave and go home. Of course, that was great news, but it also meant that Pina would have adjust to spending the rest of her stay at the jail without her friend being there with her. The next week when Ms. Gertie went to court, she was given a bond and was released that same day.

Pina received a letter a week after Ms. Gertie left. In it, she thanked us once again for making her stay in the County bearable. She sent a photo with her smiling brightly, and the caption said, "Enjoying this sweet tea in my backyard and thinking of you all."

She also stated the car rental place was working with her and had reduced the total of the cost for the car and would be writing some of it off. Ms. Gertie had to refinance her home, and her family also helped her come up with the agreed amount required to satisfy the rental company. The charges were therefore dropped and her case with them was closed. She was a free woman!

Ms. Gertie also said she had not heard from her son, and she had filed a missing person's report as well as a stolen vehicle report with the police department. She believed there must have been foul play for her son to not contact her. She asked that we continue to keep him in our prayers. She told us she would keep us posted. We clapped and celebrated Ms. Gertie's freedom and the fact we had made a small difference in the life of an innocent woman in a not-so-innocent place.

Pina and Ms. Gertie became constant pen pals and phone buddies. Ms. Gertie showed up on Pina's court date to support her and made sure there was money in her account. Who would have imagined someone's selfish ways would cause a beautiful friendship to be birthed behind bars…But God.

Love one another with brotherly affection. Outdo one another in showing honor.

—Romans 12:10 (ESV)

So we can confidently say, "The Lord is my helper; I will not fear; what can man do to me?"

—Hebrews 13:6

When the Holy Spirit Speaks

This particular day started off quietly, normal events took place, and there was nothing exciting happening. Time continued to tick by, and the women did whatever they could and chose to do to pass the day away.

Late evening, around nine-fifteen p.m., cell two received a new mate. It was quiet in the dayroom because most women were in their individual cells laying around and keeping company with others. However, as was the norm, many congregated in cell two to find out about the latest occupant. I was on my bunk preparing to settle in for the night because we only had thirty minutes or so left before we were locked in until the morning.

One of the women, Shannon, eventually went to inquire about the newbie as well, and instantly realized she knew her from outside of the jail. The women used to live in the same neighborhood and had hung out with one another. These two women were old home girls who were about to be reunited. One had no idea the other thought she was betrayed by her sister-friend, but that was soon to change. When the new person, Melanie, recognized Shannon, all kinds of chaos broke out. It went from quiet to intense in a matter of seconds. You could hear their voices raising, then the cussing began, and it was obvious that things were about to go past talking if someone did not intervene.

Shannon, who was serving three months for possession of a twenty-dollar bag of marijuana and drug paraphernalia, was going to be released in two days. However, if a person is caught fighting, that is a charge that goes on their record and their release could be, and usually was, offset.

Both ladies being repeat offenders knew this. I, however, did not know it at that time. Shannon needed to avoid this fight like the plague, but she said she could and would fight back if attacked. Melanie did not need a fight on her record either, but she knew she was going to prison because she was arrested not only for possession of crack cocaine but also solicitation of prostitution with an undercover officer…and this was her fourth offense.

Melanie accused Shannon of sleeping with her man and stealing his drugs and money before she took off and while he was cleaning himself. Melanie's boyfriend had told her this after he could not produce the product or the cash, and his boys collaborated on his story. He also told Melanie he partied too much, and Shannon took advantage of him at a party they were both attending. Melanie was then responsible to her supplier and had to work extra on the streets to pay for what the boyfriend lost, misplaced (used is more like it) or stole.

Nevertheless, Melanie convinced herself that Shannon was the perpetrator in the situation, and she had been holding a grudge ever since. It did not matter that Shannon denied the affair and stealing from the guy, Melanie's mind was made up and she wanted blood.

I am not sure how, but Shannon was able to get out of room two and make it across to her own dwelling place. Melanie had just made it into the day room when the guards opened the bars and yelled count. *Whew! Lord thank you!* Everyone had to come out into the dayroom, give their spin number and return to their cells for the night. *Glory be to God, there would be no fighting this night, not between those two at least.*

After our cell doors closed and locked, I went into night prayer as usual and went to sleep. Early in the morning, earlier than my predictable time, I was awakened with a strong yearning to pray. I turned my face to the wall while lying on my bunk and began to pray in the Spirit in my prayer language. Once I finished praying, while waiting for the Lord to speak, I went back to sleep.

I woke around eight, and went out for my routine hygiene care. Shannon was sitting up straight on the top bunk where she slept. She was looking at a magazine while rocking back and forth. As I got closer to her cell's entrance, she looked up at me and then gave me a half-crooked smile. I smiled back at her, and once I reached the point of crossing her cell door, for whatever reason I said to her, "Just breathe." I then continued on my way, never stopping.

Before I made it to the sink area, Shannon was on my heels directly behind me. She said, "Alicia, I did not do what she said."

I turned around and said, "Okay," then turned back to what I was doing. She went on to begin telling her side of the story, saying repeatedly that she was innocent and that she did not mess with Melanie's man, nor did she steal anything from him. Matter of fact, Shannon said she had not even seen him in weeks, let alone on the night in question.

"The truth will always come out," I told her. "You do not have to explain anything to me because I am not judging you. You need to be careful and try to keep peace however possible though."

"If I fight, I could lose my release tomorrow," Shannon said.

I was beginning to understand clearly what was going on. Shannon was under attack and satan wanted to steal her freedom and much more than that. "You should make sure you do not engage in any quarreling that would lead to the swinging of hands," I told her.

Shannon said, "I will not start a fight, but I will not run from one either. I will defend myself at all costs."

I could see in her eyes that she was afraid. I imagined it was at the thought of losing her release.

She then asked, "Would you pray with me Alicia?"

I prayed without delay, and she thanked me and returned to her cell quickly..

On returning to my bunk, I looked in Melanie's cell and she was asleep on her stomach. Her roommates were stirring about in the day room, and the daily movements were increasing. Because of confined quarters and a lack of a variety of activities, many women slept-in or went back to bed after they received their breakfast. Once I got back to my bunk, I began putting on lotion so I could get fully dressed and then prop my blanket as a pillow against the wall and lean back and write.

Around ten forty-five, Melanie was out in the day room cursing and cussing Shannon, saying as soon as she stepped out of her cell, she was going to bust her in the eye and stomp her into the explicative-explicative floor. It was a known fact if anything happened when someone was in someone else's cell, they would be seen as the instigator and aggressor, so that person would get in trouble and the other person would not. Melanie needed this fight to happen in the dayroom.

I skipped lunch that day and stayed in the room and snacked on commissary items, I was going to stay in the bunk and rest, no reason, just my preference. That was short-lived however, because my thoughts became consumed with Shannon's conversation with me earlier in the day. So, I began to whisper a prayer on her behalf. As I finished, I covered my head to block out the daylight and some of the sound so I could nap. That effort did not last for long. The Holy Spirit began to speak and He told me to go out into the dayroom and pray. *Really?* I remember asking silently, as I snatched the covers off and got up to go out and pray.

I made it to the first table right outside the cell. There were a few ladies finishing lunch and Melanie was sitting on one of the tables at the front of the unit. We made eye contact and she leaned over and whispered something to another woman sitting at the table with her. I began praying softly with my hands crossed and my eyes focused on them. I prayed for unity in the unit, and I began to bind and loose division, confusion, and a host of other things. I invited the Holy Spirit to have His way in the unit and asked Him to move however He saw fit.

No sooner had the words flowed from my lips than I received my next assignment. I was instructed to get up and walk around the unit and pray out loud. Without hesitation, I obeyed. I began to walk and pray, and Melanie and her table mate saw me coming. They stared in my direction, and the other ladies looked on as well.

On my third time around the unit, Melanie went into her cell. I continued praying with more volume and intensity with each trip I made. I'm not certain when, but on one of those laps I began to speak in the Spirit in my prayer language. With vigorous passion and tears streaming down my face, I surrendered my voice to the Holy Spirit. At one point my eyes were closed and my feet moved by His direction.

When I opened my eyes at some point the dayroom was empty, but the praying continued for what seemed like another ten minutes. When I was released from praying, I was at the front of the unit by the bars, and I rested my arm on the table where Melanie once sat. I just cried out for a while. It sounded like a battle cry. It was a deep, held-out "ahhh", and it changed octaves at will and went on until it did not. After silence for a minute or so, I opened my eyes again, and there was not a sound to be heard. Two ladies were standing in the doorway to their cell, and one of my cellmates was sitting at the table just gazing in my direction.

Shannon came out of her room and put some toilet tissue on the table and returned to her cell. It was then I received my next assignment. I was to go to Shannon and tell her what the Holy Ghost had just spoken to me. I immediately went to relay the message.

"Shannon," I called as I entered her room and went to her bed, "God said this is not your battle to fight. He said for you to hold your peace, that it will be over soon." Shannon began to cry and asked me if I would go tell Melanie that. I told her I would not and for her to trust God and to stand still and watch His hand at work. With that, I left her cell and went back to mine, got on the bunk, and cried. Someone came in and covered me up and I stayed in that position until I fell asleep.

I was awakened by my roommate shaking me and telling me the guard called for Shannon to get her things ready because she was leaving. Abba Father had released her from the unit! She was going home and would wait in the release tanks until they finished signing her out and returning the things she brought with her when she was booked into jail. God had delivered her from the hands of her enemy. He moved her out of the toxic situation, shut the mouth and took away the power of her oppressor.

I rose as Shannon was coming out of the cell she once occupied. She ran and hugged me and said thank you. If not for the guard standing in the unit, I'm sure Melanie would have tried to get her before she left. She was ready to pounce if given the opportunity…at least she pretended to be.

I told Shannon to thank God and for her to not come back. She agreed and left through the bars, smiling before she turned to leave. I went back to my bunk because I was drained, and pulled out my note tablet to write but before I could get a sentence completed, I went back to sleep.

That evening, Melanie was still talking noise about Shannon and all she would have done if Shannon had not left. She had an audience of two. Melanie had found those who would allow her to stroke her own ego, and that was what she desired.

I saw firsthand how God delivered His daughter. He made the impossible possible, and He made a way of escape in the wilderness. I did not know at the time, but Shannon's roommate was also praying for her, and they stood in agreement, asking God for a miracle. God has His own people everywhere; those who serve Him in places others may condemn. I have no doubt Melanie was being used by the devil and was on assignment to destroy Shannon and steal her freedom...But God had a different outcome in mind, and God always wins.

Though I walk in the midst of trouble, You will revive me; You will stretch out Your hand against the wrath of my enemies, and Your right Hand will save me.

—Psalm 138:7 (NKJV)

The Letter

One Sunday morning, while at the smaller jail awaiting my court date, I was being set up for a miracle I had no knowledge was coming; it was the Holy Spirit's doing. I had finished my morning hygiene routine, made my bunk, had breakfast, and completed my general chores. I did not do the usual rereading of my letters, instead I went into the day room, sat at the table, and began reading my Bible. That is when the thought came, *Turn on the television.*

I figured it was the devil's attempt to distract me from my personal time with the Lord, so I did not obey at first. A brief time later, I heard the thought again with the same directive: *Turn on the television.* I reluctantly did so, and to my surprise the TV was on TBN, a Christian station. Rod Parsley Ministries was on and they were having praise and worship. I quickly turned my undivided attention to the screen to watch the service.

This Sunday the message was on faith and how to move in the vein of God. It was a most interesting message and I took tons of notes on scriptures to help me gain a greater understanding of what God was saying to me in this season of my life. I believe everything we go through in life is to teach us, prepare us, and help us grow. Nothing is wasted when it comes to God, and I know He had purposed for me to hear the message.

Before ending his broadcast, Pastor Parsley asked for a seed offering. This was to be a faith offering where the participants would sow and believe God for something that seemed impossible for them to achieve alone or with their own ability. The letters would be left on the altar and prayed over throughout each day for two weeks.

Instantly, my freedom from jail became my first thought. That is exactly what I needed God to do for me, make a way for me to be released from the charges against me and to annihilate the very idea of any prison time. I was indescribably excited. I absolutely, without any doubt, knew God could do this, and I believed with my whole heart that He would.

As quickly as the happiness came, it went when the knowledge hit...I did not have the hundred-dollar seed offering he requested. I sat silently staring at the television, watching people from all over the sanctuary run to the front and place their seed money and prayer request on the altar. The phone lines were being shown and every one of them was illuminated with callers sending in their donations and prayers as well.

I sighed and looked around the room, recognizing my surroundings. Then, my eyes fixed on the opened bible on the table. Suddenly, I remembered a scripture, one that Peter had spoken, one that I was about to adopt and make my own: Acts 3:6. I went into my cell and got loose-leaf paper, an envelope, and stamps.

I began writing a letter to the World Harvest Church Ministry. It would include my prayer petition that I wanted to be added to the altar so that Pastor Parsley and his team of intercessors and prayer warriors would stand in agreement and pray with me about its contents. I knew that when two agree on earth about anything, they ask, according to His will, it will be done for them by our Father.

It came to me to let the ladies in the unit know what I was about to do and ask them if they had any petitions they wanted to include. I know that was God having me do this, and sure enough, most of the women wanted to join. I told them to write their requests out on paper and to come to my cell room so that we could petition God before mailing them off to World Harvest. I believed the more people we had praying for us and our situations the better.

My letter began with me introducing myself and disclosing my whereabouts. I then added the scripture from Acts, *"silver and gold have I none; but such as I have give I thee." Acts 3:6 (KJV).* I went on to explain that I would be praying in the Spirit so the Holy Spirit could use me to make intercession for the ministry and all the peoples' prayer submissions that had been added to the altar.

I informed the pastor that other women in the jail were also sending their petitions in by faith for a miracle as well. The letter was short and direct, I needed a miracle and so did many of the other women in jail.

The ladies began coming to where I was, one by one, with their prayer requests. They were excited and grateful they could be a part of this faith walk. After everyone arrived, we circled up and began to pray over our letters and petitions. Those who wanted to pray and make their request known aloud did so, and those who did not stood in agreement with the rest.

Once finished, we took the letter and the individual prayer requests and sealed them in an envelope. Four stamps were added to make certain there was enough postage for delivery. Shortly thereafter, we parted ways, each going back to wherever they came from and whatever they were doing.

I gave the envelope to the guard when she came through for rounds. I asked her to please make sure it was added to the out-going mail for Monday morning.

Days came and went with much of the regular schedule being implemented. However, late Wednesday afternoon things began to change. I received a visit from my lawyer, who explained they moved my court date from Thursday of the following week to this Friday, which was in two days. The judge was canceling all cases the next week because he had a pressing engagement he had to attend.

I was instructed to contact my people and persuade as many as possible to come to court that day because their support would show stability. After that piece of advice, Mr. Donaldson gathered his things to leave. Short of exiting the room, he stopped at the door and told me the D.A. had it in for me and wanted to use me as an example. He said that when I talked to my family I needed to tell them to pray, fast, burn candles, chant, or do whatever they could because I needed a miracle. He smiled this pathetic-looking weak half-grin, patted the door, and exited.

I remember questioning if he was really a "free world" attorney and exactly whose side was he truly on because it just sounded like he knew he was no match for the D.A. without Divine intervention. He seemed to know he would not win without this help. Honestly from the day I met with him, I had little to no respect for him and no confidence in his ability to argue my case. I even questioned where my family found him, and who, if anyone, recommended his services as being great, or even good for that matter, because I needed to have a serious talk with them.

Before the guard came to take me back to the cell, I called on the One who can do exceedingly, abundantly, above all I could ever ask or think. I called on and talked to my heavenly Father and made my petition known to Him. Once returning to the unit,

I made the call to my mother and eldest son and asked them to call everyone else to inform them of my new court date and time.

Friday morning, I was called out and put in handcuffs with an attached chain that led to ankle cuffs and was escorted across the parking lot to the court building. To my surprise, when I entered the courtroom, only the D.A. was present, not my lawyer, and not one person from my family, my church family, or friends were there either.

The D.A. looked at me with this smirk that conveyed to me that he thought he had this in the bag and would certainly win. I did all I could not to react to him as I was led to the chair in front of the benches. Moments later, my lawyer entered talking loudly and apologizing for being late. He said my people were caught in traffic just like he was, and would be late. He said he wanted to meet with me before court to find out a few things.

Wait, what? What could he need to find out about right before I was to see the judge? Did he not know he needed this information prior to this? What else could he possibly need to know? My thoughts whirled as my heart dropped, but I looked up toward the heavens and in my mind I said, *God I know you see this. I need You like never before to fight on my behalf.*

Less than a minute passed before the bailiff entered and told us to rise, then announced the judge. The judge entered in his black robe with a thick folder in his hand. He sat down and began to arrange his documents. The bailiff told us to be seated, and as I obeyed I looked around and still no one was coming through the doors to support me. I remember clearly thinking, *Father it does not matter if my family and friends make it today. I know there must be a good reason why they are not here. I know they love me, but you Abba Father, love me more and You are here with me. My life is in Your hands.*

It was not my first time before this judge, but it would be my last time because he was going to rule on my case and sentence me today. The D.A. requested that I be sentenced to twenty years in prison for the new charges, plus the ten years I was given previously and violated while on probation. He said because I violated my deferred adjudication probation, I was incapable of being truthful to my word to stay out of trouble and change my criminal ways. He also let the court know I had not paid the given fine either. He added that my being back in his honor's court on a violation charge proved his point.

My lawyer asked the judge to be merciful. He requested straight probation and a fine, stating that I had two young children who needed me at home. He also said I had a big family standing behind me, and the support of my church family. He also stated that I had stable employment, working with the elderly. He finished by saying that I was in a different place in my life than when the offense occurred.

The judge, shuffling through the things on his desk, looked up and asked where all the people were who came to support me the last two times. My lawyer spoke up and said they were detained by traffic, but that they were on their way and would be here like before. The judge told me to rise. As I stood, he said that he received dozens of letters and pictures from my family and friends showing support for me and speaking of my character and work ethic.

He had letters from my pastor and ministers highlighting my work in the ministry with the children teaching Sunday school, as well as being the pastor's nurse. He said, "I even received a touching letter and picture from your eldest son (which he held up), asking me to let you come home to him. I also have here a beautiful drawing from your youngest son (he was only two at the time, so the drawing was squiggly lines all over a piece of manilla construction paper)."

The Judge went on to say, "There are a lot of people that not only support you but sincerely believe in you. So, I am willing to give you the benefit of the doubt, and offer you another chance to prove yourself worthy of their trust. Therefore, I sentence you to ten years in state jail."

I nearly passed out from what I just heard. My knees were honestly buckling, and I was shaking like a leaf hanging from a tree during a coming storm. He continued, "That sentence will be enforced, and you will be arrested with an order to begin serving the time immediately if you violate any of the terms of the ten-year probation sentence I am handing down today. The terms include 250 hours of community service and a $2,000 fine."

He then said, "Those people who drove here to support you certainly have your back, and if you let them down and do not stay on the straight path, then shame on you for betraying their trust." He stood up and hit the plank with his gavel, dismissed court, and left out of the same door he had entered through.

Not completely understanding what happened, I looked at my lawyer who said, "Well, I'll be darned, he let you off with probation. You are not going to prison, well not today anyway," and he started laughing.

You can only imagine the cuss words that had surfaced in my mind. I had to quickly look to the heavens and thank the good Lord, and remember whose I was.

The D.A. walked out without gathering his belongings. I honestly do not know why he was so upset with me, but it was evident he was perturbed by the sentence I received. Now that I think about it, it probably was because my lawyer was popping his chest out like he did something.

Nevertheless, I was overjoyed, this was a huge victory for me. I told the Lord thank you aloud this time, to which my lawyer said, "Send a little thanks my way too, because I was the one doing all the work here." I thanked him but it would take God Himself to tell you how little he deserved it; he definitely was not good at representing me. This was God's doing, plain and simple. He was showing me if He be for me, who can be against me.

As the guard was taking me back to the jail, my family, church family, and other friends drove up, one vehicle after the other. When they were told the verdict by my attorney (who had the nerve to hand out his business cards like he truly was responsible for the outcome), they began celebrating. There were claps, shouts of Hallelujah, mock dancing, and hugs were freely flowing. The guard allowed it for a few minutes without interruption, and then announced they would have to come to the jail for visitation.

Once back at the jail, I was given non-contact visits to all for a few moments each. I was ecstatic. I was now and for the first time, ready to leave this small jail in Anahuac and return to the overpopulated chaos in Houston. This was a huge victory, and the next phenomenon was on its way.

Back to the letter, I do not know if World Harvest received, read, and added the letter and prayer requests to the altar or not. What I genuinely believe is that the message was intended for me and my desire to write the letter and prayer supplications activated my faith to a new level. Once the women joined with me and we prayed and thanked God in advance for meeting and exceeding our prayers, that was the trigger that activated my miracle.

I was not alone, either. Other women in the unit told of things that manifested for them since exercising their faith and joining the prayer circle that day. We believed God was able and that pleased Him. Even in the court, I was tested when my people were not there, but I told God, "But You are, and You are who I need." That pleased Him…and He showed Himself mighty and strong in that situation and in my favor.

Who knew that the simple act of obedience to turn on the television that Sunday morning would be the domino that would begin my freedom from the penial system…no one could have known …But God.

Truly I tell you, if you have faith as small as a mustard seed, you can say to this mountain, move from here to there, and it will move. Nothing will be impossible for you.

—Matthew 17:20 (NIV)

Battle of the Mind

The booking process this time did not even phase me. I knew what to expect, so I was mentally prepared for the procedures. However, this time the number of people being booked in was massive. This go 'round, I sat vertically watching and listening as the women came and went. Some were repeaters and eager to share their stories and experiences, some first-timers were noticeably withdrawn, while others were like sponges soaking up every ounce of advice anyone had to offer.

I noticed one familiar face and she recognized me as well. She asked, "Are you doing the weekend report sentence too?"

Turns out she had to report back to jail every Friday evening and was released early every Monday morning. She also stated the entire time she would be in the holding cell for the duration and learned quickly to dress extra warm and comfortably. She had to do this for four months as her sentence. This way she could keep her job and be home during the week with her three daughters. She was happy about it.

I began praying this would not be my outcome when I went before the judge. The thought of having to return to that place of doom and gloom every weekend was mental torment.

When my time came to move further into the housing proceedings, I had only one hope and that was not to be put in the Animal tank. That tank was the rowdy unit, where fights broke out, disrespect of the guards was rampant, inmates stole from one another regularly and disciplinary infractions were handed out frequently throughout the day. I was told that in that tank the women would have to strip down to their undergarments and stand in the dayroom all night because of their disrespect and unruly behavior. Those who did not have undergarments were butt-naked during this punishment phase. If male guards passed by…oh well…they had a free peep show.

The Animal tank usually housed the repeaters and those causing trouble in the holding cell. The guards could see through the small window in the holding cell door and could hear the various conversations, even though the door was made of steel. I honestly believed there was some sort of listening device in the room. I am unsure if it was because I arrived on a Sunday afternoon or what, but I was in my new unit (and thank God, not the Animal tank) in less than five hours. Signs and wonders, people…signs and wonders! I thanked God for this blessing.

I learned my court day was set for Monday the following week at nine-thirty in the morning. I called everyone and made certain they knew so they could plan on being in attendance if their schedules permitted. *One week and this could all be over!*

The tank I was put in was overcrowded and I had to sleep on the floor because all the bunks were taken in the entire unit. That alone had a huge effect on me and I began feeling trapped. Plus, everything was becoming aware to me like never before. The cold showers, bars everywhere, disgusting meals, no privacy anywhere, sour-smelling mop water...just everything. The walls were closing in on me and I physically felt like a wounded gazelle being hunted by hyenas...like there was no escape. I knew I would have to fight like never before so I would not be consumed mentally by the negativity that was coming at me from every direction.

After much prayer, I decided to go on a three-day fast that would begin on Tuesday. The strong mental attacks were monopolizing my thoughts throughout the day and seeping into my dreams at night. They were trying to destroy my faith and walk as a born-again believer.

I am not certain if you have heard it said that an idle mind is the devil's playground, but I knew that to be true and I knew to overcome the wiles of Satan I would have to fight spiritually. Fasting, praying in both my heavenly and my natural language, reading and meditating on God's words, and refraining from as much carnal activity as I could would be instrumental in my overcoming this warfare.

I wanted and needed to isolate myself but in my current environment that was an impossible desire. This mental fight was intense. I needed the Holy Spirit to intervene. There was no viable way I could manage the subtle and sometimes blatant attacks with my own strength and power.

I had to frequently remind myself of this scripture: "I do not wrestle against flesh and blood but against principalities, against powers, against the rulers of the darkness of this world, against the spiritual forces of evil in the heavenly realms," Ephesians 6:12 (NIV).

Although I knew this was happening, it was women yielding themselves to be used by the devil and I saw them and not him. *Michael, oh Michael, I need a reminder of how you taught me how to fight.* In the cell I was in, a female would use the toilet and defecate and not have the decency to flush after herself. The other females would curse and cuss her but would not flush either. It was as if I was in the midst of a bad movie, or a prank show created for the sole purpose of getting my reaction. Things were so chaotic and made absolutely no sense whatsoever.

There was nowhere to go. Every area of this unit was occupied by females. In the daytime, I would fold the thin mat I was given like a chair and sit in the corner against the wall in the cell room. My focus was diminished, and my thoughts were everywhere. I tried reading my Bible, but my mind would wander to something else. I closed my eyes to pray but some loud argument or carnal singing and chatter would not allow me to concentrate. It was utterly harum-scarum in that place.

The most peaceful place I could find was standing in the shower under the nearly warm water. That was until some of the women decided to come in and have sexy time right next to me. *Dear Lord, where is that help from the sanctuary You promised?*

Late afternoon Tuesday, out of nowhere, my name and two other names were called by the guard. We were told to gather our things and be at the gate in five minutes. All three of us were there in less than one. There were many accusations being hurled as to why they were taking us out so rapidly. There were also those who questioned us about where we were going and why. I did not know, nor did I care because anywhere else would be better than where I was…except for the animal tank.

I was nervously excited though. *Could this be over? Was my miracle manifesting at this very moment?* Yes and no. No, I was not being released to go home. And yes, instead, I was being transferred to another unit on another floor. I was happy for this win because where I was could have been classified as a den of disaster. It was a volcano waiting to erupt, a place where something major on a negative scale was bound to happen. I was grateful I would not be there in the crosshairs when that brewing thing exploded.

The new unit was much better, and I had my pick of which room I would be housed in. I chose the first one on the right, for no particular reason. My bunk was on the top this time, but I did not care—it certainly beat the floor. I settled in quickly and met my two roomies, prepared my things and puled back my blanket. I was going to turn in for the night right after the count was called, and I was excited that I would have a quiet night's rest.

Things are looking up, I thought as I readied myself for prayer and to go to sleep. The last thing I remember was telling God He was faithful and good.

I was awakened early in the morning by one of my roomies, Susan, who shook me to tell me breakfast was being passed and I needed to come and get my tray. I told her I was good, that I did not want it. She asked if I could get it and give it to her. "No problem," I said as I climbed down and honored her request.

When I brought it to her, she asked what I wanted in return. I said a thank you would be nice. She looked surprised as I set the tray next to her. She hurriedly put it on her tray and then thanked me for the food. The whole time she was eating, she was smiling like she won the jackpot or something.

Meals in the Harris County Jail were not at all appetizing. Even still, as bad as the food was, there was not enough on one tray to satisfy the hunger of an adult. Most people relied on commissaries to get them through and sustain them. Those who could not afford to purchase extra "free world" food asked for whatever another person did not want on the trays that were served. Fruits, sandwiches, and juices were especially valued items. When those delights were available and collected, the recipient considered it a great score.

With respect to commissary, peanut butter, noodles, crackers, sodas, and chocolate were the big-ticket items and would be traded for clean-up labor, sexual favors, phone privileges or whatever the holder could come up with to trade. On commissary days, the indigent women were lined up waiting to see who they could barter with, that is if they had not been pre-picked already.

Jail is a whole other place, a different world, where women do things they more than likely would not comply with on the outside. If you think what goes on in Vegas stays in Vegas is a thing, believe me it pales in comparison to what some will do in jail to stay safe, eat, or gain favor. Jail is no joke, and from what I have been told, prison is a hundred times worse.

Word came to the new unit that the previous unit I was just removed from was on lockdown, which meant no commissary, no laundry day, no phone privileges, no dayroom, and no visits. Turns out one, or some, of the women decided to clog all the outside toilets in the tank along with the drains in the shower area. Why? Who knows why. The perpetrators of these acts of vandalism caused everyone in the entire unit to be punished and locked in their cells.

The guards were demanding to know who the offenders were, and until they found out, the lockdown would continue. You can only imagine how grateful I was to God for removing me from that unit full of dysfunctional, destructive women. Whoever was guilty would certainly have additional charges, time, and fees added to their sentences, and the other inmates would make the remainder of their stay a living hell until the lockdown was ended, and possibly until they were removed and taken somewhere else.

Tuesday night was when commissary orders were due, and the items were supposed to be issued out before noon on Thursday. That deadline depended on how quick the workers and trustees were in filling the orders and how the guards felt about your unit. Even though I was on a fast, I still ordered food items to take me through the weekend. Prayerfully, I would be going home on Monday after my court case was completed. I had faith and my last win gave me another boost of encouragement.

My fasting and praying went smoothly, although I did have to fight against hunger pangs, light headedness, and much carnal activity. I stayed in the cell on my bunk most of the time, only leaving to shower and use the outside toilet.

Commissary came early on Thursday, and I honestly wished that was not the case As I stated earlier, inmates without finances who could not order things for themselves, gravitated toward those who were fortunate enough to have a package of goods coming their way. My purchase of goods put me on others' radar, and the women in need immediately came to the door with small talk and to inquire if I needed anything…anything at all. They made sure I knew they were readily available to meet whatever need I had at any time.

After politely refusing their services on several occasions, I learned that I was now a different target. I had bullseye on my back for being selfish and unwilling to help those who were destitute. What a bunch of bull. Regardless, as I told you before, jails and prisons have their own sets of rules, codes, and moral standards.

Not helping someone who offered to "work" in exchange for "needed resources" was considered wicked. It sends a message to others that the one who has and does not intend on sharing or bartering out considers themselves above not only those without but also the codes they operate under. This action makes for a hostile environment for the holder, which just so happened to be me in that instance.

Knowing this and having the desire to not be ambushed or set up in some way, I decided to comply and hire some help. Though I had absolutely nothing I needed assistance with, I contacted the first female that asked me for work, Balinda. I gave Balinda the tedious task of washing my two pairs of socks. For her hire, she was given a pack of noodles, a bag of chips, two little starburst candies and some toothpaste on an old envelope.

Now, word came back that I was showing out and trying to be big-time. *Wait…what?* Evidently, I gave too much for such a menial job. I am not making this up. Apparently, the chips and candies were over the top. Why did this make a difference? Glad you want to know. It is because now the other "workers" wanted to help me and not the other women because I knew how to show genuine appreciation.

I thought I was going to eventually end up having to physically defend myself by fighting one of the other women holding commissary. However, I did not, because Balinda let the other women know that she was the only one that would be helping me. Heaven help me, Balinda even moved into the cell with me, taking the other top bunk. Things are never as easy as they seem, though. Remember Susan, my other roomie that I gave the breakfast tray to the other day? Yep, you guessed it, she also wanted to be under my employ. Because she was already a cellmate, Balinda agreed that it would be all right. Go figure, I needed permission from the employee to hire another employee.

Susan was much quieter and more reserved than Balinda. She would smile a lot at things the others were talking about, and she would even nod in agreement or disagreement. She was not much of a talker though. Maybe this was because of her thick accent.

Balinda, on the other hand, had the vocabulary of a drunken sailor on leave. Rizza, the fourth woman in the cell with me, had her own money and could purchase her own things. She had her own hired help, Mary, who stayed in the cell across the dayroom. Rizza was pleasant and seemed to just be trying to do her three months and go home.

Inmates were coming and going, some were just arriving, some were going to prison and others to state jail or home. It was like a revolving door in that unit; as soon as one would leave, one or two new ones would come.

Things began getting iffy, with personalities clashing, bonds being shattered and confrontations on the rise. There were also a lot of threats being issued, and a sense of unrest was brewing. The women were constantly changing rooms, attempting to bunk with whomever they felt closest with in the unit. Just when it seemed as if things had settled...the trouble was only getting started.

Monday morning was court day and I was extremely excited, nervous, and anxious to get the process started. The guard opened the room doors for everyone going to court that morning, yelled our last names, and told us to be ready in fifteen minutes. There were five women from my tank going today.

It was six-thirty in the morning when they brought us out and began checking us through. Court did not begin until eight-thirty, so I already knew we would be placed in holding cells until our individual cases were called.

I was ready this time, and once we were placed in the holding tanks, I asked if anyone wanted to join me in prayer. As the women came forth or stretched out their hands, the room became silent, and I prayed for us all…including the judges, lawyers, and families.

Immediately after saying Amen, I was called out. Before entering the courtroom, my lawyer approached me and told me my case was rescheduled to a later date. The docket was full of the previous week's cases. He said my family was in the courtroom and he would let them know the new date as soon as he knew.

I tried holding back the tears, but they fell from my eyes anyway. Mr. Donaldson asked if I wanted to let them know anything. Being so choked up, I shook my head no but then mustered up the vocals to say, "Tell them I love them."

"Alrighty," he said. "Keep your head up and we will talk soon." He turned his back and exited into the courtroom without me. My knees buckled as he closed the door, and the hard breath I inhaled brought forth a feeling of utter defeat. The guard escorted me to the empty room where you waited after your court appointment, and I sat on the steel bench and cried until my nose was dripping snot, my eyes were puffed, and my throat was raw.

Other women began trickling into the holding area one by one, many with the same disappointing demeanor I exemplified moments earlier. Others acted as if it was no big deal. They were chatting and laughing, even though they knew they would have to continue to sit in jail until they saw the judge. I could only imagine those females were headed to prison and would rather continue where they were rather than go there.

Once there were about fifteen women in the room, we were taken back to the floors and units where we were being housed. I trekked the entire way as if I were walking the "Green Mile." This was horrific for me.

When I got back to the unit the assumptions began, based on the look on my face, I reckon. True to what you probably think, it was all negative. Once they found out some courts had to reschedule their docket and I was in one of those courtrooms, the bloodhounds sniffed elsewhere for their next meal and left me alone.

I made it to my cell room and climbed onto the bunk. I instantly noticed my bag with my commissary things had been opened because of the attempt at refolding it closed was terrible. The bag was rolled instead, and torn. Before I could even inquire what happened, Balinda asked why I let a crackhead come into our room and get snacks without informing my roomies.

The look of confusion on my face made Balinda jump up and walk hurriedly out of the room. Seconds later she came back in, pulling Skeeta by the arm and bringing her center stage as if she were about to recite a monologue. "Tell Alicia what you told us when you came in here," Balinda snarled.

Skeeta did not open her mouth, instead she dropped her eyes toward the floor. Susan came around quickly and got in Skeeta's face. She began clapping her hands as she spoke, and with each word, the clap became louder and more intense. "Did you not say you were told by Alicia that you could get a couple of things?"

Skeeta, who was spaghetti thin with beady little eyes and semi-matted short hair, was about thirty years old. Some of her teeth were missing and those still barely there were far from white. Skeeta stood there, rightfully afraid, in her oversized orange uniform and tried her best to come up with something to say that would get her out of the obvious trouble she had gotten herself into.

Rizza got up from her bunk, took her blanket and left the room. Balinda turned my way and said, "Alicia you should go on out to the dayroom too, you do not want to see what is about to happen. We will handle this for you."

"No," I interjected, "I want to know why Skeeta felt she had the right to enter my space and ransack my property." I was not thinking about what was just said to me because Balinda was telling me a beatdown was about to happen.

Balinda answered my question, "Because she is a thieving, feigning, lying donkey (she used the three-letter a-word instead

of donkey) crackhead who has never been dealt with properly."
With that, Susan, the quiet always smiling one, punched Skeeta
right in her face. As Skeeta stumbled backward, Susan grabbed
her by the back of her neck and smashed her face into the steel
doorway post.

Through the shock, I got down from my bunk as I told Susan,
"Stop and let her go."

Belinda got in my way saying, "She asked for it!"

As I pushed her out of my way, I could see blood on the floor.
I pulled Susan away and as I did, she kicked Skeeta in the stomach and Skeeta went down. Balinda started holding my clothes
and yanking me backward, while Susan snatched away and began
stomping Skeeta who was still on the floor in a fetal position.

I swung around and threw Balinda on the bunk, turned back
and grabbed Susan around her waist, then lifted her up, swung
her around, and stood between her and Skeeta. Balinda started
going ballistic and dapping up and congratulating Susan like she
had accomplished some wondrous feat.

Meanwhile, I turned and helped Skeeta to her feet and out
to the sink area. As expected, the other women in the unit were
gathered around speculating and volunteering their points of
view about what had just happened. They parted like the red
sea when they saw Skeeta being guided forward with blood all
over her face that was now dripping on the floor. The assembled
women acted as if they were watching a movie, and continued

gawking as they waited for one of us in that room where the mess happened to share the details about what they just witnessed.

The flowing blood was coming from Skeeta's mouth. One of Skeeta's few remaining teeth had been pushed up into her gums, while another had been knocked completely out. I'm not certain if it was from the door, Susan's foot, or both but it was surely a huge mess and one where dental attention was needed immediately because of all the blood she was losing.

No matter how I tried and tried, nothing stopped the blood. I had no choice but to call out for a guard to come. This was a risky move because of all the questions that would have to be answered. I knew this, but Skeeta was losing too much blood. Her frail little body was already weak and she could hardly stand on her own.

Sure enough, when the guard finally came, she began with the interrogation. Skeeta shut it down by saying she slipped on something wet and hit the metal table and attached round seat as she fell forward. Then for the extra effect she removed the tissue and let some blood stream out. The guard yelled for her to put more tissue in and to keep her mouth closed. I went quickly into the cell room and got her a white sock to replace the tissue. I am not certain if the guard believed Skeeta's story or truly could not care less, but what I do know is she popped that gate open and took Skeeta straight to medical.

I borrowed the cleaning towel from the mop bucket and cleaned the blood from the doorpost and sink area, I then moped the remaining blood that was on the floor. Once I returned to the room, Balinda and Susan were sitting there like proud peacocks. They began bragging to some of the women who made it into the room, that nobody was going to bother anything or anyone in our cell again. I believe they wanted me to be grateful about what had just occurred, but I was anything but that and I voiced my disapproval of their behavior. When I did this, I was called unappreciative and told if they did not handle things the way they did then any and everybody that wanted to steal from me would. They went on to say how they did my unthankful self a favor.

I climbed on my bunk and began to write a letter to my son, in an attempt to remove myself from my surroundings. That did not happen. Balinda interrupted my focus, asking, "What are we going to receive for taking care of your business?"

I know my fast worked because I did not say what I wanted to say, how I wanted to say it, instead I told her, "You are not getting anything from me because I did not ask you to do anything for me."

They both went to cussing and telling me what they should have let happen and how they could take my things if they wanted to and a whole bunch of other noise. I truly hoped for their sakes they did not try to physically come for me. That certainly would have not worked out in their favor. I think the Bible I read daily was confusing them, but before I became saved, I was nobody to play with. I had my own negative reputation and God was not through delivering me in many areas.

I looked both of them up and down and then went back to writing. Defending myself was not an issue, getting more time for fighting was however. I was in the cell where the guards could not see and if those women thought they were going to jump me, then they had another thought coming. I'm not bragging, but I would have beaten both their behinds and dared them to tell. People sometimes think because you are on the Lord's side you will let whatever happens...happen. I had not mastered that part in the Bible that says to turn the other cheek.

After talking much about what they should do, they both decided to move out of the cell room and go bunk elsewhere. That truly was the best thing they could have done.

Skeeta came back the next day with stitches in her mouth and sutures over her right eye. She kept to her story and the doctors accepted what she said without further incident. Skeeta, once she knew Balinda and Susan had changed rooms, asked if she could move into the cell. She said she was sorry for stealing and only did it because she was so hungry. Rizza said she did not feel comfortable with Balinda moving in, because this was not the first time she was caught stealing and she would not be able to rest well with her in the room.

Rizza wanted her friend and "worker," Mary to move in instead. I let Skeeta know she would not be coming into the cell room and explained why. I gave her the peanut butter she had originally stuck her spoon into (there was no way I was going to eat after her), with some other things just because I felt responsible for that serious whipping she endured. I know she should not have been stealing in the first place but, in my opinion, she still did not deserve the beating she received.

Balinda and Susan called me a fool and talked noise for a while, but eventually, other women were brought to the tank and focus shifted elsewhere. It seemed like the more carnal the tank got the more the women became excited, and soon the Skeeta drama just drifted away.

At this point, I was begging the Lord in prayer to give me a miracle of release. The walls were closing in on me and all I could do to stay sane was pray, read, and sleep. I knew the Lord heard me when I prayed, but my gosh why was He not moving? *When was I going to court? What would happen when I got there? Would I get a bond? How much longer would I be away from my sons, my family?*

I desperately wanted answers, a sign, something to help me make it through, but all I got was silence. *Why Father?* I kept asking Him. *Why aren't You saying anything?* I know during the test the teacher never speaks but this was a bit much. I was in warfare and this fight was strictly mental; good versus evil, positive versus negative, spiritual versus carnal. I could not serve two masters. This was a test of the old Lisa (what my family called me) against the new Alicia. In this situation, who would prevail? I did not even know the answer to that, no one did But God.

You will keep him in perfect peace, Whose mind is stayed on You, Because he trusts in You.

—Isaiah 26:3(NKJV)

See, I have refined you, though not as silver, I have tested you in the furnace of affliction.

—Isaiah 48:10 (NIV)

Unexpected Miracle

E arly in the morning on August 31st around nine o'clock, my name was called by an officer. Once I got to the gate, she told me to prepare for court because my name had been added to the docket and I needed to be ready to leave in the next thirty minutes. When she came back to get me, there were seven other women with her. I was number eight. *New beginnings,* I thought to myself.

The usual procedures before court were not taken this day. We had a brief pat down and a quick walk to the holding rooms outside of the courtrooms. Mr. Donaldson, my lawyer, was waiting for me when I arrived. He said he had gotten the call late the previous night about some openings and he agreed because he knew how much I wanted to appear before the judge.

He was absolutely correct, and for once I felt he had done something right and in my favor. He also said he called my mother and brother and told them to rally the troops for what could be the final showdown.

Wow! I saw him talking but my mind went into what could happen mode and I began to play out three scenarios in my head. *Best case, I would be going home to day, and the court would fine me or throw out the case or give me community service and release me and set me free. Middle line case scenario, I would be sentenced to another nine months or less in the county or state jail where I would have then been confined for anywhere up to a year and then released without further punishment. Worse case, a prison for any time over a year.*

I was snapped back to reality by Mr. Donaldson touching my shoulder and telling me that I had better pray because the bailiff would be coming to get me soon. He fixed his tie as he exited the bars and went into the courtroom. I closed my eyes, holding back the tears, and began talking to my heavenly Father in my heavenly prayer language. In my mind, I was pleading with Him to make me free.

For the next thirty minutes or so, I nervously sat there bouncing my legs at times, sitting bent over with my head in my lap at other times. But mostly I rocked back and forth, staring at everything happening and listening for every piece of hope others talked about once they exited the courtroom while on their way back to the holding cells for their return upstairs. I began wondering if anyone was able to make it to court to support me because of the short notice.

My name was shouted out by the bailiff, and I was told to line up as he opened the bars. "It's go time," he said. "You all right?" he asked as we approached the courtroom door. I told him I was, and he stopped me and said, "Pull yourself together and remember to always stay humble and respectful. You understand?"

"Yes, sir," I replied.

He went on, "You have a good judge today, this one is fair."

I could have fainted, I looked up and told God thank you as the door swung open and we entered. The courtroom was not full that day and I instantly spotted my brother, who stood up as I entered. He looked so fresh in his navy-blue slacks, baby blue shirt, and striped tie. This was my brother right under me, this brother never missed a court date. I gave him a semi-smile and he nodded at me. I could tell he was nervous too, but seeing him brought me comfort and ease. He was alone this time, but for some strange reason, I remember thinking that he was enough.

The judge, who was already sitting behind the bench, greeted me and my attorney along with the district attorney, as the bailiff left me beside Mr. Donaldson The judge read the charges against me: theft by welfare fraud.

The judge asked, "How do you plead?"

I looked at my lawyer and he nodded his head, so I said, "No contest." I was guilty of the crime, a Class B misdemeanor, because I had worked and did not report the earnings while I was receiving government financial support. My lawyer said I should plead that way, so I did. He said it was my way of saying I did not disagree with the charges against me and that I did not want to have to go into detail about how they transpired.

The judge then moved a top sheet of paper and opened my jacket (a folder that contained my charges and court information, along with any other criminal activity I might have been charged with or convicted of in the past). He looked at the D.A., Mr. Michaels, and said, "This is a misdemeanor charge (less than a thousand dollars). What is the reason for her extended stay?

Mr. Michaels quickly responded, "Your honor, she had another case pending in another jurisdiction as well."

The judge flipped through the folder in front of him and stopped suddenly and began reading. After what seemed like hours, he looked up at me, and commented, "It says here probation violation on a possession case young lady, and that carries a felony offense based on the amount seized in the original sentencing."

I stared at him without saying a word. I do not even remember blinking. My lawyer chimed in, "Yes, your honor, that is correct but based on her ties in the community, her current employment status (I was a certified nurse assistant), her church affiliation, being a single parent, and her conduct since that charge, she was given probation. Mr. Donaldson held up my Anahuac release papers with terms included. "She will also be giving back by completing community service hours at a local medical facility. Along with that, your honor, she has a fine to pay to the county clerk's office." He then offered a copy of the papers to the judge and the D.A., who acknowledged he had his own copy.

The judge looked down at his folder again, turned to the D.A. and asked, "Anything you want to add, say, or dispute?"

I could feel my legs trembling, I placed my hands at my sides, while silently screaming to myself, *Do not move!* I never took my eyes off the judge, regardless of who was speaking. To be honest, I was not sure if that was intentional.

The D.A. Mr. Michaels says, "I have nothing to add or dispute, your honor."

My lawyer, Mr. Donaldson, spoke up, "Your honor, Ms. Ceaser's brother, a Marine Corps. veteran who served in Desert Storm is here to support his sister today, and if we were not put on the docket unexpectedly last night, this whole courtroom would have been filled with other family members, church members, co-workers, and friends," he laughed. "About thirty of them, sir. They have been at all her other court hearings, showing their love and the belief they have in this young lady."

The judge looked at me briefly, "Ms. Ceaser, what is your brother's name?"

I cleared my throat, "Nelson Ceaser Jr. (truth)."

The judge asked, "Mr. Ceaser, would you stand" As he did as he was asked, the judge continued, "Do you have anything you would like to say to the court?"

Nelson stood there with his hands at his sides and his feet spread apart. "Thank you, your honor. Yes, I would like to say something."

Oh, God, I thought. *Come on, Jr., let the Lord use you.*

He said, "The woman that stands before you, your honor, no longer represents the lifestyle that you see in that folder. She has acknowledged her mistakes and has completely turned her life around for the good. She worked with senior citizens and children daily prior to her coming to jail, and the latter is voluntarily, sir. She is leading a great example before her children and they miss her terribly. I ask that she be given the opportunity to continue that path without further interruption."

I was so pleased with that moment…I was grinning and doing a happy dance inside. Mr. Donaldson blurted out my exact sentiments. *Oh my, Father,* I thought to myself. *Why don't you shut your big two-by-four lips? No one is talking to you.* My innards were boiling!

The judge said, "Thank you, Mr. Ceaser, and thank you for your service to our country. Glad you made it home…Semper Fi." They both responded, "Oorah!" With that, my brother nodded and took his seat.

This is a great thing, I thought. *The judge is probably a Marine and they just had a bonding moment.*

The judge said, "All right, Ms. Ceaser, you have been incarcerated for three months now and your other case has been finalized. We have no need to hold you any further. I am going to render a judgment of time served for the charges brought before me. Young lady, this case is dismissed. You are free to go. Return to your cell, and they will process you out when possible."

"Thank you, your honor," I said.

He nodded at me, turned to the bailiff, and said, "You can bring in the next case."

I was just standing there when Mr. Donaldson grabbed me, "Come on, girl, let's go before he changes his mind," he laughed.

I turned to look at my brother as I was being pushed toward the door by my lawyer. Jr. smiled at me and gave me a thumbs up. As I approached the holding cell, Mr. Donaldson told me he would be back with some papers for me to sign and he left as I entered the holding tank.

I was sitting there as my emotions and thoughts went everywhere. *I'm free! The case is dismissed. I am going home to my sons, my family, and my friends. I can take a hot bubble bath, eat some real food, wear my own clothes, and sleep in my own bed once again. I need to get my hair done before church because it is a mess.* I could not stop smiling or telling the Lord thank you and how great He was. I was over the top excited.

When Mr. Donaldson returned with the papers, I signed them, acknowledging the judge's decision and my agreement to the terms. *Heck yeah, the terms were the case was closed and I am being set free from these concrete walls and steel bars!* My signature was big and bold...make no mistake I agreed wholeheartedly.

As Mr. Donaldson made other comments and jokes and laughed at himself, I was thinking about how happy I was to not have to see his bug-eyed self again. As he prepared to leave, he said, "Your brother says to page him about thirty-five minutes before you are ready so that he can pick you up. I need to call your mama and let her know I did it and see if she wants to give me a bonus (he laughs loudly)." When he sees me staring at him, he stops and says, "You are a tuff one." He continued, "All right, I hope I will not have to see you again."

I quickly said, "Amen!"

"Stay out of trouble," he said.

"Will do," I said, and we shook hands before he left.

Nothing and no one could bring me down that day. I was going home, I was being released, and about to begin a new chapter in my life, one where I vowed to follow the leading of the Lord whether by His Word, His audible voice, His sent visions or dreams, or His servant-appointed watchman over my soul. I was sold out, dedicated, committed, and ready to share all that God had done for me. Who else could make my trials a steppingstone for elevation, my mess a message, or my pitfalls a catapult for success...But God. (Revelation 3:8 NLT)

I know all the things you do, and I have opened a door for you that no one can close.

—Revelation 3:8 (NLT)

Last Day

As soon the guard shut the bars, the questions began. Where did I go? Was I a witness in a case? Why did I not know I was going to court? What happened? Are you all right? And on and on. Like vultures circling a wounded animal waiting for it to take its last breath, the women in the unit were upon me from every direction.

Normally, you would not share news of your case being closed. You would not disclose that you returned only to gather your belongings and wait to be called for release. However, I felt no threat of harm and proceeded to tell my truth and to encourage, speak hope, and offer prayer. Once the ladies had their curiosity quenched and their questions answered satisfactorily or not, they moved on to something or someone else.

Some openly wondered if I would leave my belongings with anybody or would I be selfish and take them with me when I left. There was even a bet going around. I had no desire to take anything with me that reminded me of my time spent in jail. In hindsight though, I wish I had kept the commissary sheet to add to this book.

I asked my roomies if they wanted anything. Rizza wanted my Bible and a Smiths Wigglesworth book I had. Mary, who worked for Rizza, asked for a few stamped envelopes and one of my writing tablets. I gave both ladies what they requested.

Skeeta, the one who stole from me and was beaten down, came to the door and asked if she could please have everything I was not going to take with me. She gave her best plea of how she had nothing and nobody to visit or put anything on her books, and that she was all alone. I did not give her everything, but I did give her some things, which included a pair of socks and a t-shirt. The latter, I supposed, she would sleep in because it certainly would swallow her up because our sizes were quite different.

Once I finished with Skeeta, I went over to Balinda and Susan's cell and asked if I could speak with them. They invited me in and offered me a seat on one of the bottom bunks. I thanked them and told them I wanted them to know I understood why they responded the way they did with the whole situation with Skeeta and her stealing. I knew there were lines you did not cross, and rules set that carried difficult and harmful consequences if disregarded or not followed. I told them I would have liked it if things were handled differently but I understood why it was handled the way it was.

I also thanked them for having my back and for standing up for me and apologized for the way I responded. I let them know that I was aware that it seemed as though I was unappreciative and that was because I honestly did not want to see anyone hurt nor did I want to see anyone catch another case because of me.

Balinda asked, "Why did you not say that then? Why were you angry with us?"

My response was, "I did not like violence over what I considered to be petty theft."

They told me if the petty theft was not dealt with, then it would have been a major theft the next time and that there would have been a next time because anybody that wanted to take something from me would do it because there were no consequences.

"You are right," I told them. "But I honestly was trying to avoid trouble and chaos at all costs. I was doing my best to live peaceably with everyone."

Susan stated, "Living peaceably does not happen here. Someone would target you for that very reason and you would have to eventually prove yourself and defend yourself. If you did not, then you would be easy prey for those looking to come up or establish rank, authority, and position."

"I know that, and I am no pushover. Even though I wanted to avoid trouble, I would not sit idly by and allow physical harm to come upon me, I would protect myself at all costs. I would defend myself if I have to, but I did not look for disturbances.

Though I would not flee from any that knocked at my door with ill intent."

The two ladies made jokes, and called me the silent reaper, the quiet one-hitter quitter, the innocent ender. I laughed with them and just like that, the beef was squashed and we were okay.

I told them I would be leaving (they already knew) that day and I wanted to give them some things I had set aside for them. They said they wanted them and told me thanks. I asked if I could have their spin numbers (the number given to identify those in jail and prison) so I could keep in touch and add money to their accounts once I left. They both willingly and hurriedly obliged.

I gave them two bags that contained lotions, powder, toothpaste, soups, candies, writing tablets, soda, cookies, chips, pens, playing cards, and socks. They both were grateful and vowed to share things equally. I honestly believe what Balinda and Susan wanted most was for me to acknowledge that they had my back and that I appreciated what they had done. They changed their whole demeanor once I apologized for my behavior toward them. I do not care who or where you are, everyone wants to be respected.

I learned many things during my time in jail. That is that things will not always be ideal and people will not always act according to one's hopes. Different circumstances hold different consequences with which you may not agree. I learned that you cannot expect others to submit to your way of doing things just because you want them to because you think it is the best way because it is your belief. Everyone is responsible for how they react and handle various situations.

Most importantly, I learned that various places have their own sets of laws and rules that must be adhered to. These are the rules that add structure and maintain order in that setting and location. The Correctional System is not where I would advise anyone to aspire to going because it is a whole other way of living. Jail is not understood by those who have never had to do any amount of time there. While it has and serves its purpose, the objective should be to avoid this growing industry at all costs.

I did my time, paid my debt to society, and came out wiser than I went in. Jail is no walk in the park, by any means, but it was the biggest wake-up call I had experienced at up to that time.

I was called to gather my things four hours after my court case ended. It took another two hours to process me out. During the wait of about an hour in the release tank, I called my mom to let her know I was on my way home. I asked her to page my brother and put the number 35 so he would come for me and bring me to the house.

There are some kind and decent people in the penal system. Some made a wrong decision and got caught. Some were desperate and could not see another way and got caught. Some reacted wrongly and got caught. I fell into one of those categories and had to pay the piper. Many of you were fortunate enough not to have gotten caught in your wrongdoings but would have ended up in the system if you had been caught. I loudly echo the cliché: "If you cannot do the time, then do not do the crime." It honestly is not worth the risk.

I made it through, though not on or in my own power and strength. I made it because I surrendered to the leading of the Holy Spirit, did what was required of me, stayed out of the readily available drama and troubles as much as possible, and stayed in the presence of God. Yes, His presence is there in jail as well. Because He is with me always, I survived and thrived through a challenging time in my life. I say without a doubt I survived because of nobody's help But God!

If I ascend up into heaven, thou art there: if I make my bed in hell, behold, You are there.

—Psalm 139:8 (KJV)

Closing

It is my sincerest hope that this book is used to expose the enemy's lie where one believes because of any ungodly circumstances they are marked for failure. I hope the light of truth bursts forth to inform or remind you that God can and will bring good out of your situation and life if you allow Him. I hope you remember that you were predestined with a purpose and as long as there is breath in your body that divine design is still attainable.

No matter where you are...God is...and He wants to use you as His vessel to uncover untruths, invoke awareness, and reveal His love. You, beloved, have the opportunity to do kingdom-building work as God's holy ambassador. Just as you are and just where you are. Right now, you are where He needs you to be...to reach those He needs you to reach.

It has taken me over twenty-five years to write this book. The events you read about happened in 1997. Yes, I was a procrastinator and thought my story could not possibly make an impact on others. It is my earnest prayer that this revelation jolts like a lightning bolt into your consciousness and you begin to search yourselves.

If you have used your testimonies, your talents, and gifts to the glory and honor of God, I salute you. If you know there is more that you could and should do, I implore you to let this be the day you begin. If you have not realized you have a calling and assignment, I assure you that you do and the master planner, God Himself, wants to disclose that to you.

You, my brothers and sisters, are unique, peculiar, and one of a kind. Only you can thoroughly and effectively complete the tasks you were given before the foundation of the world. You can make a positive difference in the lives of others just by being your true, authentic self. Please seek your platform and help bring about someone's healings, deliverances, and/or their breakthroughs.

It is in your hands and outside of you...no one will know if you choose to go forward and pursue your purpose or if you choose to remain stagnant and keep surviving instead of thriving...no one that is But God!

Selah,
Alicia

About the Author

Alicia Ceaser, a native Houstonian, born-again believer, and single parent is determined to share the gospel through her writings. She is an international playwright, author of nonfiction adult and children's books, and actress both on stage and in film. She teaches and directs theater arts where she molds and cultivates the minds of future generations through the world of plays and skits. She gives students the full experience on stage and behind the scenes.

She also writes and directs full-scale productions and skits for churches and communities. Additionally, she writes personalized and generic poems as well as gospel lyrics. Her purpose is to use her life experiences and God's Word to bring Him Glory and expose the wiles of the kingdom of darkness. She seeks to shine light and Godly truth while exposing the enemy and his devices.

Her pen and computer are her weapons of choice. Determined to fulfill her destiny by using her God-given talents and gifts to expand His Kingdom, she vows to leave a legacy of writings that can bring light into every dark place it enters. For that she is grateful.